D1408434

Lexie's Gift

A COOKBOOK FOR KIDS LIVING WITH CANCER

Lexie's Gift

A COOKBOOK FOR KIDS LIVING WITH CANCER

Lexie's Gift ©

A COOKBOOK FOR KIDS LIVING WITH CANCER

MOON LADY PRESS

575 Summer Street
Marshfield Hills, MA 02051

First Edition printed January, 2014

ISBN-13: 978-0-9753473-6-2

To order printed and/or electronic copies:
visit The Magical Moon Foundation
www.magicalmoon.org

The information provided in this cookbook is not meant to diagnose, prevent, treat or cure any disease or illness.
It is essentially a collection of recipes created to reduce the consumption of fermented, mold susceptible,
inflammatory, processed and high glycemic foods, and is supported by related information.
Always consult your physician and nutritionist regarding your cancer treatment and diet regimen.

Sir Lexie Legend of Love

An Invitation from Lexie

Hi! My name is Lexie Williams, and I am a Knight of the Magical Moon.

I've had a brain tumor since I was a baby, and by the time I was 9 years old I had already had two brain surgeries and two chemotherapy protocols. Now I am 15 years old and I am Sir Lexie, The Legend of Love, a real Knight with a real sword and real armor, living with cancer. Like all Knights I have a mission, mine is to write a cookbook for kids with cancer so that all the kids who are diagnosed can change the way they eat to fight their cancer. So I started my quest by looking for healthy foods easily prepared so that all kids like me will have some yummy recipes to help them feel better and keep them healthy. Many of these recipes contain a healthy and delicious spectrum of vegetables, fruits and fresh herbs, highlighted by the healthy "Eat the Rainbow" color that they represent. Some of the recipes in this cookbook boost our immune systems, some provide energy, some lift our spirits and help us to build up our strength, some settle our stomachs or soothe our worries, and all just plain taste good.

I could never have gotten this mission off the ground without the love and support of my fellow Knights of the Magical Moon, the Moon Spoon Team, and some very special friends.

Georgia Manzo Joachim has authored a cookbook of her own and is my chief cook and advisor extraordinaire. Georgia worked painstakingly on the recipes in this book for three years, testing, tasting and testing again to get it right.

iv

Mark Mincolla, Ph.D., a renowned nutritionist, taught me that food is medicine, and that I can maintain the chemical balance in my body by eating the right foods to fight my cancer.

Donna Green, excecutive director of the Magical Moon Foundation, created the Magical Moon Farm, where I became stronger, more independent, and more self- confident.

There are my fellow Knights and their families. In our journey to get better, we have the support of our siblings every single day, and they deserve a chapter of their own. So we put together some recipes for them, our quiet heroes.

And then there are Angel Knights; Sir Kyle and others, whose favorite recipes and/or thoughts on cooking and eating are featured in a very special chapter of this cookbook.

There is much more too, including gluten-free foods, fun snacks, meals for all seasons, and my favorite – pasta recipes!

Kids who have cancer go through many different stages of treatment and sometimes certain foods don't taste very good, while other foods are craved; so we've added a chapter that offers recipes that have worked for us during and following our chemothera-py treatments, and we hope they work for you too.

We Are Warriors! And warriors need to stay healthy and strong to ward off the diseases that sometimes invade our bodies and our lives. What we eat is one of our greatest weapons in our quest for good health. So let's raise our swords and start our journey. Enter the Knights' Magical Kitchen, and believe in yourself!

Lexie's Gift

A COOKBOOK FOR KIDS LIVING WITH CANCER

Sir Lexie's Dedication

This cookbook is dedicated to Angel Knight, Sir Kyle the Cook (Kyle Kerpan). Kyle was my friend and had the same kind of tumor I have but his wouldn't stop growing and he passed away. Kyle loved his cookbooks and he loved to cook. It made him happy and brought him peace. With limited ability to read, the pictures provided him with a vehicle to take him to a safe place where he could talk about and share his favorite recipes with others. He especially loved Rachael Ray's cookbooks and she signed every one of them!

The following is an excerpt from Kyle's mom's journal of his illness, his legacy, his light and his strength:

"Our son Kyle was diagnosed with a brain tumor when he was 2½ years old. He lost his long fight when he was 11... During these years he learned to live around his tumor not with his tumor. He did not live in fear of his life but in love with his life." And further, in speaking of the hardships of his illness…"He did it with grace, with trust and with undoubting hope. In his short life, he met Phil Collins and he met Rachael Ray and he brought a smile and a laugh to all those around him…he brought a peace and calm to his illness…Kyle's Peace…a peace to now be shared with others who continue this fight alongside him…"

Read more of Kyle's history by visiting
www.caringbridge.org/pa/kyledkerpan/history.htm

We raise our swords to you, Sir Kyle, and celebrate your spirit and your love for cooking in the recipes that follow.

Contents

Contents

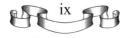

What Guides Us

Mark Mincolla, Ph.D., markmincolla.com, is a revered nutritionist and natural health care practitioner who has transformed the lives of thousands of people over the past 30 years with his knowledge that food is medicine. On his website he quotes Dr. Otto Warburg, Physiologist and Nobel Laureate, who discovered that:

"Cancer, above all other diseases, has countless secondary causes. But even for cancer there is only one prime cause. Summarized in a few words, the prime cause of cancer is the replacement of the respiration of oxygen in normal body cells by a fermentation of sugar."

In essence, cancer feeds on sugar and fermentation. With this information as a guide, Dr. Mincolla inspired us to transform traditional childhood favorites to make them safer yet keep them delicious, and to create appealing new recipes sure to become favorites. Here's how you can do it.

Eliminate all processed sugars including molasses, corn syrup, maple syrup, honey, and cane sugar. Other foods to be strictly avoided include: breads with yeast, vinegars (and all foods containing vinegar such as some mustards – read the label), beer, wine, champagne, nuts (especially peanuts, cashews and pistachios), mushrooms, morels, truffles (any fungus foods), aged cheeses (mold), soy sauce, miso, tempeh and tamari, and dried or tropical fruits including melons.

Eliminate all inflammatory foods. There are foods that contain a fat called arachadonic acid. This fat drives up COX 2 enzymes that trigger the body's expression of eicosanoid prostanoid hormones that contribute to inflammatory disease. When you inhibit these hormones, you inhibit cancer cell growth. **Inflammatory foods to be avoided include:** pork, red meat (unless it is grass-fed and limited in the diet) farm- raised fish, tilapia, dairy (milk, egg yolks, cheese, yogurt, cream cheese, sour cream), fungal susceptible corn products and all nuts except for walnuts, soy nuts, macadamia nuts, and occasionally, almonds (and those must be fresh). Also avoid processed carbohydrates, processed sugars, fermented foods, and nori seaweeds.

Increase consumption of certain foods: wild salmon, halibut, sardines, lake trout, tuna, free-range poultry, non-fermented soy products, fresh pumpkin, flax, chia seeds, sesame seeds, sunflower seeds and dark greens. Liberal use of turmeric, rosemary, oregano and Ceylon cinnamon is encouraged for their anti-inflammatory support. **Most** vegetables and fruits are neutral and acceptable.

Limit consumption of fresh fruit: Cancer can adapt to fruit sugars when deprived of highly processed sugars, so eating no more than one serving of fresh fruit a day is recommended. Whenever possible, fresh fruit juice should be consumed within 20 minutes of juicing (or frozen in air-tight containers) to reap the benefits of the healthy enzymes in juice that are oxidized with prolonged exposure to air. These enzymes are what break down the fruit's sugar. **Limit bottled fruit juices and never use bottled fruit juices that contain added sugar.**

Some good foods to eat: Salads are good with EV olive oil and lemon dressing. **High fiber starches** such as barley, brown rice, multigrain, low glycemic or gluten-free pasta, quinoa pasta (as long as it is corn-free), oats, and sweet potatoes are good. **Drink green or white tea, ginger tea, and 60-plus ounces of water a day (preferably distilled).**

Unsweetened dark chocolate 60-70% or better, **sea salt, egg substitutes** such as Egg Beaters® and **trans fat free butter substitutes made from natural oil blends** such as Earth Balance® or Smart Balance® are fine except for baking. **Ghee** is okay and great for baking. **No-yolk noodles** are okay too.

This is not an all-inclusive list, but provides a fairly comprehensive pattern of foods to embrace and avoid.

In the end, we are empowered by knowledge; and the more we have the more we are able to create wonderful meals that children love while eliminating the environment in which cancer cells thrive... and that is what this cookbook is about.

In this chapter,
some of my fellow knights
will introduce themselves and
tell you their stories of

love, courage and hope.

- Lexie

Lady Hailey Knight of Hugs

"Hi, my name is Lady Hailey, Knight of Hugs. When I was about a year old, I was diagnosed with a Pilocytic Astrocytoma in my brain stem. I am now 15 years old and have had five brain surgeries, with one that resulted in paralysis down my right side. I've had ten other surgeries. When I was two years old, I underwent radiation and am now on my eighth course of chemotherapy. For the past two years my tumor has been stable and not growing.

My mission is to help my friend and fellow knight, Sir Lexie, with her cookbook. I agree with her one hundred percent that there should be a kid-friendly cancer cookbook. The chemotherapy medicine that I am on is making my cholesterol levels really high, so I've been trying to eat better. I believe that this cookbook will help us and other kids eat healthy and have a good time doing it."

Hailey (Giguere) is a humble knight, full of stamina and love. You'll never meet anyone with more grace and courage than Lady Hailey, Knight of Hugs.

Sir Callie the Conqueror

"My name is Sir Callie the Conqueror. I was diagnosed with Acute Lymphoblastic Leukemia (ALL) on October 16, 2010 when I was 10 years old. I am now 13, and as I write this, I have just finished some of the more intense aspects of my treatment. When I was first diagnosed I was in the hospital for 6 weeks. My initial phase of treatment took longer than expected because I ended up getting a bacterial infection in my brain which I battled for months.

Having this experience has made me look differently at my life. I realize now that I am stronger than I ever expected. I never thought I could make it through all the different procedures and take so much medicine!

I try to stay positive and I know that even though this has happened to me, I will take this experience and turn it into something good. I have chosen my knight's mission, using my art to help endangered sea life. But I know that I also want to help other kids with cancer feel strong and know that they aren't alone. I know we will conquer this disease together."

Sir Callie the Conqueror, Callie Herschfield, is working with Donna Green at the Magical Moon Farm to build an art and music therapy room in the barn for children with cancer.

Sir Christopher Knight of Joy

"Hi, my name is Christopher Bartorelli. I was diagnosed at the age of seven with an Anaplastic Spinal Ependymoma (Stage 4). Since that time I have had two spinal surgeries, radiation treatment and am still undergoing weekly chemotherapy treatments at the Jimmy Fund Clinic.

I have had the occasional break in all of this, usually lasting all of about a month each because of the aggressive nature of my tumors. It is very hard for me as there are only a handful of children out there diagnosed with this type and location of cancer. Therefore the doctors are just guessing at my treatment. Right now my treatment is working but the future still remains uncertain.

That being said, I do not let it get me down. I am 16 now and live my life to the fullest every day. My biggest joy is my ability to work with the younger children, whatever they may be doing - to mentor them and help them become the best that they can be. I spend a lot of time volunteering to help the kids in our Little League program. I am a member of the National Junior Honor Society at my school and I am on the committee for a program called Rachel's Challenge. This is a 'Pay It Forward' program. Rachel Joy Scott was one of the victims in the Columbine shooting and this was her goal. As a member I am also able to tell my story as well as those of my friends fighting cancer. I believe that not only are children our future, but they are destined to stand together to achieve great things. I have many great friends to help me carry our message and hopefully bring more awareness to our plight."

During all of this Sir Christopher continues to smile, mentor, and just be a good friend no matter what the situation.

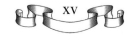

Sir Luke Collection Knight

"My name is Luke Ronco and I am 12 years old. I was diagnosed with a brain tumor on my optic nerves and my hypothalamus when I was three years old and had lots of chemotherapy and proton beam radiation therapy. My tumor is inoperable and sometimes it grows and sometimes it behaves, as my mom likes to say. I lost a lot of vision so I have been learning Braille for the last 6 years.

When I was in the hospital, my mom gave me my first Pez dispenser. I enjoyed playing with it, but when I was five years old, I really started collecting them. I have about 2000 Pez dispensers now and hope to add more to my collection.

My mission is not only to encourage kids to use collections to help them with a difficult situation the way this hobby has helped me, but also to encourage kids and adults to recycle the many things we have around us and re-purpose them for another use. Do you compost? It is great for the earth and the waste dumps. Do you have a recycle can at your house? It is an easy thing to do! Don't forget ways to re-use other items too, like cardboard and scraps of fabric. You can be really creative. A bunch of kids and I even made an animal zoo from recycled items. Please get on board and support my mission!"

Luke is an amazing young man who is helping to build a healthy Earth Kingdom where children don't get cancer!

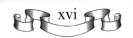

Sir Michael Knight of the Magical Sun

"Hi, my name is Sir Michael, Knight of the Magical Sun. I am 11 years old and I am a brain tumor survivor. On April 8, 2004, I was diagnosed with an ATRT (Atypical Teratoid/Rhabdoid Tumor). I was four years old. I had brain surgery the day I was brought to the hospital and then had 12 intensive weeks of chemotherapy and later a 10-hour brain surgery to remove the tumor. As part of my protocol, I had six weeks of intense proton beam radiation to my brain and spine and another six months of maintenance chemotherapy. I ended treatment on January 25, 2005.

Being a knight of the Magical Moon has been a lot of fun but it is serious too. I am a real knight and being a real knight, I have a real mission in my life. Actually I have two.

My first Knight's mission is to help sick children to look at the sunnier side of things. Because of what I've been through, I want to help give strength and courage to others. My mantra is, "Never, Never, Ever, Give Up!" I love life and I've learned to never take anything for granted. I visit kids in the hospital and I assure them that they are strong enough to get through it. I tell them that if they can find a way to turn lemons into lemonade, they will become much stronger and get well faster. Then I give them one of my bottles of lemonade with my picture on it. It is called Sunshine Lemonade and is 100% natural with very little sweetener, no preservatives and no artificial colors added. It's the best lemonade you'll ever taste!

My second mission is to encourage people to use solar heating in their homes. The sun is very powerful and generates a lot of natural energy that doesn't pollute the earth or give kids cancer."

Thank you, Michael Lanosa, for your positive message and your Sunshine Lemonade!

Sir Sammi — Thriving Survivor Knight

"On March 27, 2003, I was diagnosed with a brain tumor. I was ten years old. They found the tumor because it had burst inside my head and caused Chemical Meningitis. The tumor was removed 16 months later during a four hour-long craniotomy. It was found to be benign.

It's now just a couple weeks before my 18th birthday. I've had to deal with many after-effects of the tumor and the treatments for it. In the last eight years, I've had a total of 38 surgeries. I have to take about a dozen pills and two to three shots a day. I've had dozens of MRIs and CAT scans and countless blood draws, IVs and finger pokes along with thousands of X-rays; and I've spent months in the hospital.

I haven't been able to attend school in years and that's why the Magical Moon Foundation is so important to me. The Magical Moon Foundation is all about my fellow Knights and me; and Donna's farm is where we get to just be with each other and talk about the things we want to change. We all have missions that we want to put into action and Magical Moon is helping to give us a voice so that people can start to listen. My personal mission as a Knight is to write. I'm working on a book that I've tentatively titled "Benign My Butt" because even benign brain tumors can be life threatening and extremely harmful. Besides my book, I also sometimes write essays, letters and speeches to help people understand how serious brain tumors and cancer in kids are and also how common they are, contrary to what most people think. Last year, I even shaved my head to raise money and awareness for Childhood Cancer research and then went on national TV, along with my mom and 44 other women from all over the country!

I won't stop until my mission, and the missions of my friends at the Magical Moon are accomplished. I won't stop until pediatric cancer and brain tumors are as distant a thing of the past as medieval knights and as seemingly mythical as dragons."

Sammi Robertson home-schooled herself since 7th grade and recently graduated with her GED – in the 90th percentile!

Sir Scotty the Strong and Serene

"Hi! My name is Scotty Davidson (Sir Scotty, the Strong and Serene). In June of 2007 I had an accidental fall down my basement stairs. After a visit to the emergency room, where my parents thought I would be treated for a broken shoulder, I was diagnosed with an inoperable brain tumor. The technical term is optic chiasm/hypothalamic glioma. I finished 70 weeks of toxic chemotherapy in October of 2008. During that time I suffered hair loss, leg pain, severe nausea, low blood counts, and hospitalizations. Needless to say we were happy when it was all over!

The trial study I participated in seemed to be a success for me. My tumor underwent a 70 percent volume loss and my first "off treatment" MRI showed stability. Then in March of 2010 after being off treatment for 18 months I discovered that my tumor had progressed in two areas. I am now on a protocol of chemo with four different agents for one year. I go every two to three months for eye exams to watch my peripheral and central vision loss. This is related to the location of my tumor, being in the optic chiasm.

I also am currently receiving Lupron injections every 28 days to lower my testosterone level – again because of the tumor's location, being involved with the hypothalamus portion of my brain.

Even through all these appointments and big medical terms, I live my life to the fullest each day. I enjoy being nine years old, playing with my dog, riding my bike, shooting my BB gun, and catching a ball."

Scotty is a warrior of the truest fashion! He handles his journey with so much grace and strength that he is a hero to all who know him.

Sir Stephanie the Strong

"I'm Sir Stephanie the Strong. At age two, I was diagnosed with stage 4 Wilms' tumor that metastasized from my kidneys to my lungs and lymph nodes. I've gone through nine surgeries, and I'm still going through the long-term side effects of the treatments. Every day is a battle, but with the love and support from my friends and family, I manage to overcome each obstacle one day at a time.

For as long as I can remember, I've wanted to become a Pediatric Oncology Nurse; so I decided to incorporate my life-long dream into my mission as a Knight of the Magical Moon. I know it's a tough field to be in, but I always knew I had something more to offer than the average person with the desire to be a nurse - I have a story of survival to share with the world. I feel that my place in the medical field is alongside the children who are suffering, as I once was. I want to take care of them and help them keep their faith so they too can continue fighting. I believe it is crucial for them to have someone who knows exactly what they're going through to help to keep their spirits up. I would love to be that person, by their sides, helping them overcome each of their battles day-by-day.

And even though I know there will be some who won't make it, I will make it my duty to keep going strong, because one day cancer will no longer overpower us. WE WILL OVERPOWER CANCER!!!"

Stephanie Torres' goals are strong and she will someday be the caring pediatrics nurse she always wanted to be. In many ways, she already is!

Sir Thomas Knight of the Shooting Star

"Hello, my name is Sir Thomas, Knight of the Shooting Star. I am 6 years old. I have Nonketotic Hyperglycemia, NKH, a rare incurable metabolic disease. I also have Primary Immunodeficiency, PID, which is a fancy way of saying I have a poorly functioning immune system. The treatment that would help my PID cannot be used because of my NKH. I spend a lot of time in and out of the hospital.

My mission as a Knight of the Magical Moon has been to help raise money and find a cure for NKH. My mom and I started the NKH Crusaders Foundation. I have met a lot of amazing people and I want to help other children who are fighting NKH."

Many thanks go to brave knight Sir Thomas (Thomas Archibald) and his mom, Kristen, for their dedicated quest to find a cure for NKH!

Choose Certified Organic...
and other important guidelines for parents

These symbols may be found in various recipes throughout the cookbook:

 A little spicy (**Some kids are sensitive to spicy foods at different times and for different reasons. Reduce, substitute or eliminate spices as necessary.**)

 Contains steps that may be done the day before to save time or that require 2 or more hours of prep time

 Divide and freeze portions for use at a later date (**Breads in this cookbook may be divided and frozen in portions to accommodate later use as bread crumbs or sandwich slices, and soups are easy to thaw and re-heat when a quick comfort food is needed.**)

Also throughout this cookbook you will see notes and special hints specific to the recipe. Some important broader guidelines are described below along with key comparisons regarding safe alternatives.

- Choose **Certified Organic** where there is a choice and if possible, grow some of your own organic foods. Organic ingredients are usually more expensive, but the true cost of not buying organic is the toll that the treated pesticides, commercial fertilizers and hormone/antibiotic-fed poultry and meats takes on our bodies, and on our planet in the form of unhealthy soil and the amount of fossil fuels used in production. On the following pages, **Affording and Stocking Your Healthy Pantry** offers possible resources for obtaining organic and alternative ingredients at a reasonable price.

- Use free-range, all natural poultry, and grass-fed bison and beef.

- Always thoroughly rinse fresh fruits, vegetables, herbs and poultry before preparing.

- In most cases, cooking and baking oils used in the following recipes will be canola oil (expeller-pressed, organic) such as Spectrum® brand, or extra virgin (EV) olive oil. You will also see recipes that include toasted sesame oil and EV coconut oil. Ghee is butterfat that has been separated from the water and milk fat proteins and is used in some of our recipes as well as buttery spreads made from natural oil blends (a good source of Omega 3 essential fatty acids) and that do not contain hydrogenated or partially hydrogenated oils.

- Recipes requiring eggs will call for egg whites. You may choose egg whites or all-natural egg substitute depending upon your child's need for protein, but we will refer to egg whites only in the recipes that follow. One-quarter cup of egg substitute (made with egg whites and added protein) equals one egg in liquid content and contains 6 grams of protein. An egg yolk contains approximately 2.7 grams of protein. An egg white contains around 3.6 grams of protein. Always be sure the egg substi-

tute you are using is made from egg whites, such as Egg Beaters® brand and always check the date for freshness.

- Glycemic Index (GI), simply put, is the rate at which food is converted into glucose. Carbohydrates with a high GI break down quickly and rapidly release glucose into the bloodstream.

- Organic coconut nectar or crystals (neither taste like coconut) and barley malt syrup (be sure ingredients list is simply organic sprouted barley and water) are the primary sweeteners used in this cookbook in place of refined table sugar that has a glycemic index of about 68. Coconut nectar and coconut crystals, (that in our experience taste better than brown rice syrup) have a GI of about 35 and the natural fructose content is very low as compared to some sweeteners including agave nectar. The ratio of coconut nectar/crystals to refined table sugar is 1:1 so there need not be any rebalancing of ingredients in recipes that traditionally call for table sugar. Barley malt syrup has a GI of about 45. Its taste is similar to molasses and its ratio to refined table sugar is 1.3:1, so use 1⅓ cups barley malt syrup where you would ordinarily use 1 cup of table sugar. Additionally, reduce another liquid in the same recipe by ¼ cup. When barley malt syrup is replacing honey or molasses in a recipe, there is no need to alter other liquid contents as the ratio is 1:1.

- Flours used include a blend of white/whole wheat, oat, amaranth, rice, tapioca and spelt, among others such as are in the all-purpose gluten- free mixtures. As you get more comfortable with these recipes, try adding less white flour and more of the other less processed flours.

- Soy, rice and coconut milk are used in place of dairy milk. Vegetable cheeses such as Galaxy Nutritional Foods® Pepper Jack, Swiss and Mozzarella do not contain partially hydrogenated oils, sugar or vinegar and are used in place of dairy cheeses in our recipes.

- Baking powder used in the following recipes should be cornstarch-free, such as Hain Featherweight® brand.

- Liquid aminos seasoning, such as Bragg® brand, is a non-GMO, non-fermented soy protein, and is used in place of soy sauce in our recipes.

- Acceptable thickeners used in piace of cornstarch are tapioca starch, kudzu root starch or arrowroot starch. Ratio to corn starch is as follows respectively:

  Tapioca starch (thickens quicker than corn starch) – 2:3 (2 teaspoons of tapioca starch to 1 tablespoon of corn starch)

  Kudzu root starch (superior in jelling strength, taste, and healing qualities but more expensive than arrowroot or tapioca) – 4:2 (4 teaspoons kudzu root starch to 2 teaspoons corn starch)

  Arrowroot starch/flour (not preferable for milk-based sauces or meat sauces – gets a bit slimy) – 1:1 (1 teaspoon arrowroot starch to 1 teaspoon corn starch)

Affording and Stocking your Healthy Pantry

Cooking with organic foods and healthy ingredients may seem pricey, but you can lessen the impact on your pocketbook by shopping at your local farmers' markets where many great deals are available, or at organic food stores. To find markets and stores near you, go to www.farmland.org/americas-favorite- farmers-markets-states.asp, www.ams.usda.gov/farmersmarkets/ and www.organicstorelocator. com/.

There are also food co-ops everywhere that offer reasonably priced products and ingredients due to their practice of buying in bulk. You might want to consider growing your own products at home or sharing space in an urban community garden. Check out www.localharvest.org or www.coopdirectory. org/directory.htm to find a co-op near you; or for a very comprehensive site for all things organic near you visit www.organicconsumers.org.

Other resources include various large chain supermarkets, whole foods and natural foods stores (look for sales), and online resources such as www.amazon.com, www.vitacost.com, and www.iherb.com. These on-line stores often feature sales and special offerings including free shipping.

Other solutions:

- Buy in bulk when prices are low and freeze or store until later use. Plan your menu around ingredients that are on sale that week.

- Combine organic with non-organic purchases if prices are simply too prohibitive to buy entirely organic. When buying organic, focus on those vegetables and fruits that would otherwise have the most pesticide treatment such as apples, strawberries, celery, peaches, spinach, grapes, potatoes, lettuce, kale and sweet bell peppers.

- Save on other items by clipping coupons, buying clothing and other items at thrift shops, and being conservative with other household expenses in order to spend more on organic food products.

- Buy frozen versions of organic foods such as berries and fish. They are usually less expensive than fresh.

- Eat with the season as our grandparents did. Foods are less expensive when in season.

- Always plan your menu and check your supplies before going to the grocery store to create a succinct list of needs – and never go grocery shopping when you're hungry!

- Check the "Unit Price" and compare. Most grocery or retail stores provide the unit price and it typically shows how much you're paying per ounce in the package size options available.

Following are some of the dry goods, natural sweeteners, oils, stocks and flavorings used in our recipes that you may want to stock in your pantry (organic whenever possible):

Butters, Fats & Oils:
- Expeller-Pressed Canola Oil
- Extra Virgin Coconut Oil
- Extra Virgin Olive Oil
- Expeller-Pressed Toasted Sesame Oil
- Ghee
- Soy Nut Butter

Baking Products:
- Bittersweet Chocolate Chips
- Vanilla Extract – Alcohol Free if possible
- Unsweetened Shredded Coconut

Binders & Leaveners:
- Baking Powder (*free of Cream of Tartar or Corn Starch*)
- Baking Soda
- Gaur Gum
- Xanthan Gum

Broths & Sauces:
- Liquid Aminos Seasoning (*such as* Bragg®)
- Low-Sodium Chicken Broth
- Low-Sodium Vegetable Broth

Dried Herbs, and Spices:
- Cayenne Pepper, Ceylon Cinnamon, Chili Powder, Cumin, Curry, Dillweed, Ginger, Herbes de Provence, Dry Mustard, Parsley, Rosemary, Sage, Sea Salt, Thyme and Turmeric

Flours:
- All-Purpose Gluten-Free Flour Mix
- Oat Flour
- Oat Pastry Flour
- Quinio Flour
- Rice Flour (*Brown & White*)
- Spelt Flour (*Whole & White*)
- Tapioca Flour
- Whole Wheat Flour
- Whole Wheat Pastry Flour

Pasta & Rice:
- Couscous
- Gluten-Free Pasta (*assorted*)
- Low Glycemic Pasta (*assorted*)
- Multigrain Pasta (*assorted*)
- Rice Noodles
- Brown Rice

Seeds & Nuts:
- Chia Seeds
- Macadamia Nuts
- Poppy Seeds
- Pumpkin Seeds
- Sesame Seeds
- Sunflower Seeds
- Walnuts

Sweeteners:
- Barley Malt Syrup
- Coconut Crystals
- Coconut Nectar

Thickeners:
- Arrowroot Powder
- Guar Gum
- Kudzu Root Starch
- Potato Starch
- Tapioca Starch

Read the labels. Some items may need to be refrigerated after opening. In the case of certain flours, be sure they are well-sealed and used by expiration date.

Other chilled stock items include:
- Buttery Spreads (*made from healthy oil blends*)
- Coconut Milk
- Egg Substitute (*all natural*)
- Fresh Eggs (*use whites only*)
- Fresh Herbs (*Basil, Cilantro, Dill, Oregano, Parsley, Rosemary, Sage, Thyme*)
- Lemons, Limes
- Rice Milk
- Soy Milk
- Vegetable Cheeses (*Mozzarella, Pepperjack, Swiss*)
- Vinegar-free Mustards

Eat the RAINBOW!

It's so important for kids to eat colorful foods. The more **naturally** colorful the food, usually the better it is for us. So the way we can help ourselves to get all the vegetables and fruits that we need is to think about EATING THE RAINBOW! If we eat something with each meal that is a color from the rainbow (**red, orange, yellow, green, blue, indigo, violet**), we are making ourselves healthier and stronger.

Below is a partial list of some of the healthy and colorful foods that should be part of our daily diet and are highlighted throughout this cookbook in the rainbow's healthy spectrum:

Red: tomatoes, beets, apples, cherries, radishes, raspberries, red beans, red cabbage, red grapes, red pears, red peppers, strawberries, watermelon

Orange & Yellow: apricots, bananas, carrots, garlic, nectarines, onions, oranges, peaches, pears, sweet potatoes, tangerines, yellow and orange peppers, squash

Green: asparagus, avocados, broccoli, Brussels sprouts, celery, cucumbers, edamame, fresh herbs, green beans, green cabbage, green grapes, green pears, green peppers, kale, kiwi fruit, lettuce, peas, spinach, zucchini

Blue/Indigo/Violet: blackberries, black currants, blueberries, blue potatoes, eggplant, plums, purple grapes, purple peppers

The Negative Rainbow of Food Dyes

Food dyes are some of the most widely used, potentially dangerous additives and are found in a myriad of consumed products. The information surrounding food dyes is varied and plentiful. We advise parents to educate themselves to the possible effects of various food dyes and to consult with their child's nutritionist about the potential health risks associated with each of them.

Some of the most common food dyes used today:

Blue #1 (Brilliant Blue) is found in baked goods, beverages, dessert powders, candies, cereals, drugs, and other products.

Blue #2 (Indigo Carmine) is found in colored beverages, candies, pet foods, and other foods and drugs.

Citrus Red #2 is used to color the skins of Florida oranges.

Green #3 (Fast Green) is used in various drugs, personal care products, cosmetic products, candies, beverages, ice cream, sorbet, and ingested drugs.

Red #3 (Erythrosine) is found in sausage casings, oral medication, maraschino cherries, baked goods and candies.

Red #40 (Allura Red) is the most-widely used and consumed dye. Red #40 is found in beverages, bakery goods, dessert powders, candies, cereals, foods, drugs, and cosmetics.

Yellow #5 (Tartrazine) is used in pet foods, numerous bakery goods, beverages, dessert powders, candies, cereals, gelatin desserts, and many other foods, as well as pharmaceuticals and cosmetics.

Yellow #6 (Sunset Yellow) is in colored bakery goods, cereals, beverages, dessert powders, candies, gelatin desserts, sausages, cosmetics and drugs.

Breads & Basics

The homemade breads in this chapter are delicious and fun to make. Parents may freeze these breads in serving portions for later use.

If you're having a busy week, and need to buy yeast-free and/or gluten-free bread instead of making it from scratch, an available brand is EnerG® yeast-free, gluten-free Brown Rice Bread. Go to http://www.ener-g.com/yeast-free-brown-rice-loaf.html. Buy and freeze loaves in sections for bread crumbs or school sandwiches. (Other yeast-free breads are available, but try to avoid varieties that contain corn products or vinegar.)

Using chilled ghee helps to make these biscuits fluffy because large particles of cold ghee create air pockets when baking, thus making a flakier, lighter biscuit than one cooked with softened ghee that makes a more paste-like dough.

Billowy Biscuits

Makes 12 biscuits

1½ cups white spelt flour

1½ cups whole wheat flour

1½ teaspoons sea salt

½ teaspoon baking soda

1 tablespoon baking powder (cornstarch-free)

¼ teaspoon granulated garlic

½ cup plus 1 tablespoon chilled ghee, cut into small pieces

1 cup plus 2 tablespoons rice or soy milk with 2 tablespoons lemon juice

- Preheat oven to 450°F. Sift the dry ingredients (including granulated garlic) together into a mixing bowl. With a pastry cutter, cut in the ghee until the mixture feels granular and the ghee is the size of small peas. Add the rice or soy milk with lemon juice.

- Mix dough lightly and roll out onto a well-floured work surface. Knead lightly 10-12 times, flouring as needed. Flour the rolling pin and roll out to ¾-inch thickness. Cut with biscuit cutter and place on ungreased or parchment-lined baking sheet, close together but not touching.

- Bake for 16-18 minutes or until biscuits are golden and cooked through. Place on wire rack to cool or serve warm.

Breads & Basics

Did you know that blueberries promote healthy eyesight? Serve this luscious syrup over our pancakes or our chocolate bundt cake. Substitute blueberries with raspberries, strawberries or blackberries if you prefer.

Bionic Blueberry Syrup

Makes 2 cups

3 cups fresh or frozen blueberries

½ cup coconut nectar

1 teaspoon lemon juice

Pinch of sea salt

Pinch of Ceylon cinnamon

1 tablespoon kudzu root starch or arrowroot starch

2 tablespoons cold water

- In small saucepan, combine blueberries, coconut nectar, lemon juice, sea salt and Ceylon cinnamon. Place over medium heat and stir. In a separate small bowl, mix the starch with the water to make a slurry. Add the slurry to the blueberry mixture and stir. Bring to boil. Remove from heat, stir again and let stand 5 minutes. Serve warm.

- May be made ahead, refrigerated and reheated, or frozen in covered ice cube trays and used as needed.

Cut into desired size for sandwiches or as a side for your favorite soup or salad.

Fantastic Focaccia

Makes 1 (9 x 13) pan

1 batch Billowy Biscuits dough (page 29) with ¼ teaspoon dried basil
   and ¼ teaspoon dried oregano
EV olive oil for drizzling
Chopped fresh or dried rosemary leaves for sprinkling
Coarse sea salt for sprinkling

- Preheat oven to 450°F and line a (9x13) baking pan with parchment paper. Turn the seasoned dough onto a well-floured surface and knead lightly. Place in baking pan and spread to edges with small rolling pin or with floured hands. With your index finger, poke holes in the top of the dough (1 inch apart), drizzle with EV olive oil and sprinkle with chopped fresh or dried rosemary leaves and coarse sea salt.

- Bake for approximately 15-17 minutes. Place on wire rack to cool completely while still in the pan. Cut to desired slices.

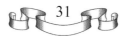

Breads & Basics

This basic yeast-free flatbread could have many variations. For example, following this recipe is a Southwestern variation with chili powder and ground cumin that makes a great taco shell. Or make it plain with no seasonings or with just a little sea salt. The resting and kneading is very important to activate the glutens, especially since there is no yeast. This flatbread is fun to make and great with your favorite sandwich ingredients rolled up inside! Or, tear the flatbread into pieces and dip the pieces in warm tomato sauce. Or make Stone Pizza (page 181) with this dough. To freeze individual flatbreads, completely cool and stack between layers of waxed paper before wrapping in freezer bags in individual meal portions.

Flying Saucer Bread

Makes 8-12 flatbreads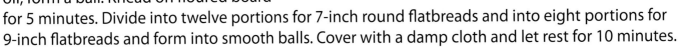

1½ cups whole wheat flour
1½ cups unbleached, all-purpose flour
2 teaspoons sea salt
¼ teaspoon dried basil
¼ teaspoon dried oregano
¼ teaspoon dried thyme
1¼ cups warm water
2 tablespoons EV olive oil
EV olive oil for griddle pan

- Combine the flours, salt, and dried herbs in a bowl. Stir in water and olive oil; form a ball. Knead on floured board for 5 minutes. Divide into twelve portions for 7-inch round flatbreads and into eight portions for 9-inch flatbreads and form into smooth balls. Cover with a damp cloth and let rest for 10 minutes.

- Meanwhile, heat a griddle pan on medium to medium low heat (for softer flatbreads). Press each ball flat and roll out on a floured board to make desired sized circles. Lightly oil the heated griddle pan with EV olive oil and place one of the flatbread rounds on griddle and cook for about 1½ minutes per side. You may have to add a little olive oil off and on and regulate the griddle temperature during the process of cooking all the flatbread. Place flatbreads on a rack to cool.

- **Southwestern version:** Replace the basil and oregano with ½ teaspoon chili powder and ½ teaspoon cumin. Prepare and cook on griddle pan as above.

Fresh basil is a good source of beta-carotene, Vitamin A and iron. It contains anti-inflammatory and anti-bacterial properties, and when steeped in tea, basil helps relieve nausea. This pesto may be frozen in covered ice cube trays or freezer containers for later use. When thawed, it will darken considerably but will still taste great.

Fresh Basil Pesto

Makes I cup

2 cups packed fresh basil leaves, rinsed and dried

I clove garlic

¼ cup plus I tablespoon pine nuts

¼ cup silken tofu, well drained

⅓ cup EV olive oil

½ teaspoon sea salt

⅛ teaspoon freshly ground black pepper

- Combine the basil, garlic and pine nuts in a food processor and pulse until coarsely chopped. Add the tofu. Slowly add EV olive oil and process until smooth.

- Season with sea salt and black pepper to taste. Refrigerate for up to 1 week.

Breads & Basics

The trick to this rustic bread is in not over-handling it, and preheating the oven and cast iron pan 20 minutes before cooking. This bread is a yeast-free staple for many recipes. Freeze sections of this bread to use for stuffing, fresh or dried bread crumbs and for your meatloaf and meatballs. See below for instructions to make dried breadcrumbs (used in several recipes in this cookbook).

Irish Soda Bread

1 cup white spelt flour

1½ cups whole wheat flour

1½ cups unbleached, all-purpose flour

1 tablespoon baking powder (cornstarch-free)

1 teaspoon sea salt

¾ teaspoon baking soda

6 tablespoons cold ghee

¾ cup chopped plums or grapes (optional)

4 egg whites (divided)

1¼ cups rice or soy milk with 2 tablespoons fresh lemon juice

2 tablespoons barley malt syrup, slightly warmed

- Preheat oven to 350°F. Place a cast iron pan (8-inch diameter) in the oven to preheat.

- In a large bowl, combine the dry ingredients. Cut in ghee until mixture resembles coarse crumbs. Stir in chopped plums or grapes. Set aside one tablespoon of the egg whites. Add the rice milk mixture, the warmed barley malt syrup and remaining egg whites to the crumb mixture; stir just until flour is moistened (dough will be sticky). Turn onto a well-floured surface; knead lightly and quickly about 10 times. Shape into a ball.

- Remove the hot cast iron pan from the oven and place a potholder or oven mitt over the handle so that you don't forget that it is very hot. Using a pastry brush, and with quick strokes, grease the bottom and sides of the pan with 1 tablespoon EV olive oil. Place the dough into the hot pan and place in oven and bake for a total of 1 hour and 10 minutes. During the last 20 minutes of cooking, cover the loaf with aluminum foil. Cool for 10 minutes before removing from pan to a wire rack to cool completely.

For Dried Breadcrumbs

Preheat oven to 350°F. Place 2-3 cups of small-cubed Irish Soda Bread or other yeast-free bread cubes in a single layer on a parchment or foil-lined baking pan. Sprinkle cubed bread with 2 tablespoons EV olive oil and 1 heaping teaspoon dried Herbes de Provence or dried Italian seasoning. Turn with hands to meld oil and herbs; bake for 10 minutes. Turn with spatula and bake 5 more minutes or until crisp. Remove from oven and set aside to cool. When cooled, grind into bread crumbs and place in airtight container until ready to use.

Breads & Basics

Energy-boosting, tasty and versatile...this spread has it all. Try it on flatbread or as a dressing for your sandwiches; use it as a roulade filling or tossed with your favorite pasta. This spread may be frozen in covered ice cube trays or freezer containers for later use. When thawed, it will darken considerably but will still taste great.

Kick-It-up Kale Spread

Makes 2 cups of spread

1 bunch fresh raw kale leaves, stems and spine removed
1 (15-ounce) can low-sodium chick peas, drained
½ cup pine nuts
2 cloves garlic, minced
½ cup EV olive oil
Juice of one lemon
½ teaspoon sea salt
⅛ teaspoon freshly ground black pepper
½ teaspoon ground turmeric

- Rinse and thoroughly dry the kale. With kitchen shears, cut off stems and spines. In two or three equal portions, place kale leaves in food processor and chop to a fine consistency. (A large bunch of kale is probably too large to place in food processor all at once.)

- Place the first batch of chopped kale leaves back into the food processor with the second batch. Add the remaining ingredients and pulse until pureed. Add a little more EV olive oil or some water a teaspoon at a time if mixture is dry.

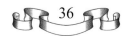

This recipe was perfected with the help of a young man named Michael Buda who wanted to share in the adventure of this cookbook. This ketchup may be frozen in covered ice cube trays or freezer containers for later use.

Kool Ketchup

Makes 1¾ cups ketchup

1½ cups tomato puree (from fresh tomatoes - see process below)

1 (6-ounce) can tomato paste

½ cup coconut crystals

1 teaspoon sea salt

½ teaspoon onion powder

½ teaspoon ground mustard

⅛ teaspoon ground allspice or 3 allspice berries, crushed

⅛ teaspoon freshly ground black pepper

⅛ teaspoon granulated garlic

Pinch ground cloves

Pinch Ceylon cinnamon

1 tablespoon lime juice

1 teaspoon kudzu root starch or arrowroot starch/flour

2 teaspoons water

- Pulse 3-4 medium very ripe tomatoes in food processor until pureed. Place bowl under fine mesh strainer and strain pureed tomatoes, pushing pulp through until there is very little left. Discard remaining pulp. Place remaining strained puree into a 2-cup measuring cup (should equal 1½ cups puree). Pour puree into medium saucepan. Add remaining ingredients except lime juice, kudzu root starch or arrowroot starch/flour and water. Whisk until smooth. Bring to a boil, reduce heat to low and simmer for 45 minutes, uncovered. Add lime juice and stir.

- In a small bowl, combine the kudzu root or arrowroot starch/flour with the water and blend. Add to tomato mixture and simmer for another 15-20 minutes until thickened. Remove from heat. Store in refrigerator for up to 1 week or freeze for up to 3 months.

Quick & Tasty Tomato Sauce

Makes I quart sauce

¼ cup EV olive oil

I large onion, diced

I red bell pepper, seeded and diced

2 ribs celery, finely diced

3 cloves garlic, peeled and chopped

I (28-ounce) can ground peeled tomatoes

I (28-ounce) can tomato puree

I (6-ounce) can tomato paste

½ cup water

I teaspoon sea salt

¼ teaspoon freshly ground black pepper

2 teaspoons Herbes de Provence

- In a heavy saucepan or skillet on medium heat, sauté the diced onion in the olive oil until caramelized (about 15 minutes). Add the red bell pepper, celery and garlic and sauté for 10 minutes on medium low. Add remaining ingredients, cover and simmer 45 minutes, stirring occasionally. Adjust seasonings to taste.

Savory Stuffing

Serves 4-6

3 tablespoons EV olive oil

1 small onion, diced

2 ribs celery, diced

1 apple, peeled, cored and diced

3½ cups fresh breadcrumbs from Irish Soda Bread (page 35) or other yeast-free bread

2 pre-cooked, all-natural chicken sausages, finely chopped

2 tablespoons pine nuts or sunflower seeds

1 tablespoon each chopped fresh rosemary, thyme and sage, or 1½ teaspoons dried poultry seasoning blend

½ teaspoon sea salt

¼ teaspoon freshly ground black pepper

Pinch of red pepper flakes (optional)

1½ cups low-sodium chicken broth

3 tablespoons ghee

- For fresh bread crumbs, place slices of bread in a food processor and pulse.

- On medium heat, sauté diced onions and celery in the olive oil for 10 minutes.

- Add the diced apple and sauté another 3 minutes. Transfer to a large mixing bowl and allow mixture to cool. Add the remaining ingredients except for the chicken broth and ghee. Stir lightly to blend.

- Preheat oven to 350°F. In a saucepan, heat the chicken broth and ghee until ghee is melted. Pour chicken broth mixture over the stuffing mixture and fold gently to combine all ingredients. Spoon the stuffing into a casserole dish that has been lightly greased with EV olive oil. Mixture should be a little on the wet side since some of the moisture will be absorbed as it cooks. Cover and bake for 40 minutes. Let stuffing sit covered for 10 minutes before serving.

Breads & Basics

Try these breadsticks dipped in Quick & Tasty Tomato Sauce (page 38).

Skinny Fingers Breadsticks

Makes 12 breadsticks

½ cup oat flour
½ cup unbleached, all-purpose flour
1½ teaspoons baking powder (cornstarch-free)
1 teaspoon sea salt
½ teaspoon granulated garlic
⅔ cup soy or rice milk
1½ tablespoons ghee, melted
1½ tablespoons EV olive oil
Sesame seeds for sprinkling

- Preheat oven to 450°F. Combine dry ingredients and gradually add milk to form a soft dough. Transfer to floured work surface and knead gently 5-6 times.

- Flouring the work surface again, roll and shape the dough into a (10 x 5) rectangle. Cut into 12 sticks.

- Combine the melted ghee with the oil and pour into a large baking dish or jelly roll pan. Place uncooked breadsticks in pan, turning gently to coat them. Sprinkle with sesame seeds. Bake for 12-15 minutes or until golden brown and a little crispy on the outside. Serve warm or cold.

Super Spelt Sandwich Bread

Makes 1 loaf

½ cup flaxseed (soaked in ½ cup water)
4 cups white spelt flour
1 teaspoon sea salt
1½ teaspoons baking soda

⅓ cup barley malt syrup
2 cups rice or soy milk
2 tablespoons EV olive oil

- Soak the flaxseed in ½ cup water for 2 hours. Do not drain.

- Preheat oven to 350°F. Line a loaf pan with parchment paper or grease with olive oil.

- Place flour, sea salt and baking soda in a large mixing bowl and stir to blend. Add soaked flaxseed and remaining ingredients. Using a wooden spoon, stir briskly for 1 minute. With rubber spatula, pour mixture into prepared loaf pan. Bake for 1 hour and 15 minutes, covering the loaf with aluminum foil in the last 15 minutes of baking. Insert toothpick or cake tester to check for doneness. Cool completely before slicing.

- Store this bread in refrigerator for up to one week. Freeze in portions for later use.

For a change of pace, try this spread on your Rainbow Wraps (page 188) in place of Terrific Tomato Dressing.

Tofu Cream Cheese Spread

Makes 1½ cups

1 cup silken tofu
1 tablespoon coconut nectar
1 tablespoon rice or soy milk
½ teaspoon lemon juice

1 teaspoon sea salt
¼ teaspoon freshly ground black pepper
1 small clove garlic, minced
½ cup pine nuts or sunflower seeds

- Squeeze liquid out of tofu through a clean white (lint-free) dish cloth. Place all ingredients in small food processor and pulse until creamy. Chill for at least 2 hours.

Double this recipe for a standard (9 x 13) lasagna pan.

Tofu Ricotta Filling and Pizza Topping

Makes 2 cups

1 (14-ounce) package extra firm tofu
2-3 teaspoons fresh lemon juice
2 teaspoons EV olive oil
1 medium clove garlic, minced
10-12 fresh basil leaves, chopped
½ teaspoon sea salt
¼ teaspoon freshly ground black pepper
Pinch of nutmeg
1½ cups shredded vegetable mozzarella cheese
1 egg white (only when using this recipe as filling for pasta dishes)

- Drain the tofu and press it into a strainer to release more moisture. Squeeze it between your fingers, breaking it up completely, and press again. Add the lemon juice, olive oil, garlic, chopped basil, sea salt, pepper and nutmeg. Mix again and press slightly. Add the shredded vegetable cheese and fold until blended. Add egg white (except when using this recipe as pizza topping).

- Sprinkle on your favorite pizza or fill a lasagna, stuffed shells or manicotti..

Eating During Chemotherapy or After Surgery

Coping with Side Effects

Lexie says, "Things I did to deal with the side effects of treatments were to eat what tasted good if certain foods tasted badly or if I was nauseous. I would drink lots of water to prevent constipation caused by dehydration, and I would treat myself to dark chocolate candy at the end of the day if I drank my whole water bottle. When I felt tired I would just lie on the couch and rest and when I felt good I would get up and try to have some fun. When I was hot or tired the nausea and fatigue would get much worse. Once I vomited for 17 days straight and all I could eat was my friend Larry's pasta with sauce, and Mr. Lindo's pizza."

(For Italian Flag Pizza, see page 121, for Stone Pizza, see page 181.)

According to the Children's Brain Tumor Foundation, www.cbtf.org, changes in (or difficulties with) nutrition can occur in children with tumors. After surgery, children may experience temporary nausea and vomiting. Taking steroids can cause a dramatic increase in appetite. Children undergoing radiation therapy or chemotherapy often develop irregular eating patterns or nausea or complain that their foods taste metallic (like tin), are too salty or too sweet, or even have no taste. They may lose their appetite, have a feeling of fullness, or have diarrhea, cramps, constipation or dry and/or sore throat or mouth. Cancer can place extra nutritional demands on the body and change how nutrients are used. Always consult your child's physician and nutritionist/dietician before giving your child vitamins, herbs, alternative supplements, or before starting a new diet regimen. Certain compounds can interfere with cancer treatment and can cause harm.

When your child isn't eating well, you're less likely to overreact if you understand that there will be "off" eating days. Appetite will probably improve over time, and an "on" day is an opportunity for you to increase the nutritional value of the foods you're preparing. Food is closely tied to emotions, so try to avoid confrontations over meals.

Recipes in this chapter target these appetite fluctuations and will hopefully provide your child with the nutritional needs, the tummy soothers, the fatigue fighters, the foods just for fun, and the return to normal eating habits that are so important during and after surgery or treatment.

Recipes to Feed Our Needs

Children with cancer need protein to grow and repair tissue, maintain healthy skin, blood cells, the immune system, and the lining of the digestive tract. Your child's cancer care team and nutritionist will help you to determine specific needs at specific times. Lean meats, fish, poultry, legumes, soy foods, and seeds are good sources of protein.

Carbohydrates will provide fuel for your child's organs to function properly. How much is needed depends on your child's size, age, and level and amount of physical activity during and after treatment. Good sources of carbohydrates are vegetables, fruits, whole grains, brown rice, dried beans, peas and best of all – avocados.

A child being treated for cancer may need considerably more calories than other children. Healthy fats and oils such as extra-virgin coconut oil are also a rich source of energy (calories). They provide more than two times the calories per gram than carbohydrates.

Trout is a mild and delicious fish - especially brook trout! It is full of essential Omega-3 fatty acids and is loaded with protein, vitamins and minerals. Have it in this refreshing salad, or served warm with Soothing Smashed Potatoes (page 75) and steamed spinach.

Fishing Derby Salad

Serves 6

3 fresh small to medium brook or lake trout (not farm raised), cleaned
Whole wheat flour, sea salt, and freshly ground black pepper for coating
2 heads Romaine lettuce, chopped
6 green onions, chopped
10 Sun Gold or red cherry tomatoes cut in half

Citrus Dressing

¼ cup canola oil
1 tablespoon fresh lemon juice
1 teaspoon fresh orange juice
2 teaspoons coconut crystals
½ teaspoon sea salt
Sprinkle or two of hot sauce (optional)
2 teaspoons chopped fresh chives

- Preheat oven to 400°F. Coat skin side of trout in mixture of flour, sea salt and freshly ground black pepper. Place in oven-proof baking pan coated with canola oil. Roast for 15-20 minutes or until fish meat flakes off easily with a fork. Remove from oven, allow fish to cool enough to handle; de-bone thoroughly and remove skin.

- Rinse and dry vegetables and place in salad bowl. Drizzle salad with Citrus Dressing and top with trout pieces. Serve at room temperature or chilled.

The Republic of Tea® makes a green tea with peppermint variety called "Moroccan Mint" (Tea of Good Health) that works well in this recipe, but there are many delicious varieties of peppermint tea available.

Green Tea Power Punch

Makes 1 quart

2 cups hot water

6 green tea with peppermint tea bags or loose tea equivalent in infuser

3 tablespoons coconut nectar

½-inch chunk fresh ginger, peeled and sliced

1 tablespoon fresh lime juice

1 tablespoon fresh lemon juice

2 cups sparkling water

Crushed ice

- Place the tea bags or tea-filled infuser, coconut nectar and ginger slices in the hot water. Stir and cool completely. Remove the ginger and tea bags or infuser. Add the lime and lemon juice, top with sparkling water and crushed ice when ready to serve.

Mama Mia Meatballs with Quick & Tasty Tomato Sauce

Serves 4-6

Meatballs

1 pound grass-fed ground bison

2-3 thick slices Irish Soda Bread (page 35) or other yeast-free bread

Water for soaking bread

4 egg whites

3 medium garlic cloves, minced

1 teaspoon sea salt

¾ teaspoon freshly ground black pepper

1 tablespoon dried parsley

Pinch of dried thyme

Pinch of cayenne pepper

1 tablespoon EV olive oil

- Place the ground meat in a large bowl. In another bowl, soak the bread in the water, one slice at a time; squeezing out excess water and crumbling the bread slices (approximately 1½ cups in total) into the bowl with the ground meat. Add the remaining ingredients and mix with your hands. Do not over mix.

- Preheat oven to 400°F. Coat a shallow baking pan with 2 tablespoons EV olive oil. Form the meatballs into 2½-inch balls and place onto prepared baking pan in a single layer. Bake for 20-24 minutes. Serve drenched in Quick & Tasty Tomato Sauce (page 38) with your favorite pasta.

Open Sesame! Brussels Sprouts

1 tablespoon toasted sesame seeds
2 pounds Brussels sprouts
1 teaspoon toasted sesame oil
Sea salt and freshly ground black pepper to taste

- To toast sesame seeds, place them in a small, ungreased skillet on medium- high heat and cook, stirring occasionally with a wooden spoon until just lightly browned or until they start "popping" and are fragrant. They will burn quickly so must be watched closely and should only take a few minutes to toast. Remove from heat and set aside.

- Rinse and drain Brussels sprouts; slightly trim and discard ends. Place water in bottom half of steamer and Brussels sprouts in top half of steamer. Cover and steam for 7-10 minutes or until tender but still bright green. Remove from heat and place Brussels sprouts in a serving dish; drizzle with toasted sesame oil and sesame seeds and season to taste with salt and black pepper. Serve immediately.

Pumpkin "Fricassee"

Serves 4-6

2 tablespoons ghee
2 medium carrots, finely diced
½ yellow bell pepper, seeded, trimmed and finely diced
I small onion, finely diced
I small zucchini or summer squash, finely diced
I (I5-ounce) can pumpkin (I00% pure), or 2 cups cooked fresh pumpkin
I¼ cups unsalted vegetable broth
I (I5-ounce) can diced tomatoes
I teaspoon fresh chopped (or ¼ teaspoon dried) rosemary
¼ teaspoon paprika
Sea salt and freshly ground black pepper to taste
¾ cup multigrain, low-glycemic or gluten-free macaroni or fusilli pasta
¼ cup shredded vegetable mozzarella cheese

- In a large saucepan on medium heat, melt the ghee and sauté the diced carrots, bell peppers and onion for 5 minutes, stirring occasionally. Add the zucchini or squash, cover and continue cooking for 5 more minutes. Add the pumpkin, stir to blend; cover and cook on medium low heat for 10 minutes, stirring occasionally to prevent sticking.

- Add the vegetable broth, diced tomatoes, rosemary, paprika, sea salt and black pepper. Cover; cook on medium heat for 20 minutes, stirring occasionally. Remove from heat.

- Meanwhile, in a separate saucepan, bring 3 cups of water to a boil, add the pasta and cook for 9 minutes or until al dente. Drain and add the pasta to the pumpkin mixture, stir and transfer to a serving bowl and sprinkle with vegetable mozzarella cheese. Serve immediately with your favorite salad.

Eating During Chemotherapy or After Surgery

Fatigue-Fighting Foods

Being tired is one thing, but fatigue associated with cancer and its related treatment is much different. With cancer fatigue, you can feel tired even if you've had a good night's sleep. You may experience any of the following symptoms as you live with fatigue during cancer treatment:

- "whole body" tiredness
- tiredness that continues even if you have rested
- becoming tired even with simple activities, such as walking to the bus
- difficulty concentrating
- feeling like crying, or being overly emotional or sensitive
- getting tired very quickly instead of it happening slowly throughout the day
- not wanting to do the things you used to like to do.

Some of the causes of this fatigue are:
- the cancer itself (changes in metabolism, pain, low oxygen level)
- the treatment you are receiving (chemotherapy, radiation, surgery and medications)
- difficulty eating (loss of appetite, mouth sores, or taste changes)
- the day-to-day stress of living with cancer.

Always talk with your oncologist and health care team including your nutritionist about being tired (even between appointments if you notice changes).

Mitochondria, the "power plant" of our cells, create more than 90% of the energy needed by the body to sustain life and support growth. When mitochondria fail to function properly for one reason or another, organs and tissues can have an "energy crisis". Organic leafy greens, seeds, sweet potatoes, dark chocolate, raspberries, cherries, chicken, grass-fed bison, egg whites, green tea, wild cod, haddock, sardines and salmon are a sampling of foods that contain the minerals, vitamins and other nutrients that help to keep mitochondria healthy. Talk with your health care team about other energy-boosting foods and possible supplements.

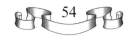

Cherries and Elderberries contain the phytonutrient anthocyanin. Though studies are ongoing, it is believed by many scientists and nutritionists that the chemical compounds in anthocyanins help our bodies prevent and fight diseases and pain because they have been shown to have anti-inflammatory, anti-viral and anti-microbial properties.

Black Cherry Green Tea Booster

Makes one cup

1 cup boiled water

1 green or white tea bag

1 tablespoon unsweetened Black Cherry or Elderberry concentrate

- Place boiled water in tea cup or mug; add the tea bag and black cherry or elderberry concentrate. Stir; steep for 3 minutes. Remove tea bag and enjoy, or chill and serve over crushed ice.

Eating During Chemotherapy or After Surgery

Grass-fed bison provides the protein boost that is so important following chemotherapy treatments.

Magical Moon Meatloaf

Serves 6-8

I pound ground grass-fed bison

1¼ cups fresh yeast-free dried breadcrumbs (for Irish Soda Bread crumbs, see page 35)

I tablespoon mustard (vinegar-free such as Coleman's®)

⅓ cup finely diced red or yellow onion

2 cloves garlic, minced

2 large egg whites

½ cup rice or soy milk

2 teaspoons liquid aminos seasoning

I teaspoon sea salt

¼ teaspoon freshly ground black pepper

1½ teaspoons fresh (or ⅓ teaspoon dried) thyme

1½ teaspoons fresh (or ⅓ teaspoon dried) oregano

⅛ teaspoon cayenne pepper

- Place 2-3 slices yeast-free bread in a food processor and pulse until coarse crumbs.

- Combine all ingredients, by hand, in a large bowl – do not over mix. Preheat oven to 350°F. In a shallow baking pan, form meatloaf by hand into an oblong loaf about 8 inches long by 4 inches wide, with a flat top, or place in loaf pan.

- Cover evenly with Meatloaf Topping (below), or with ¾ cup Kool Ketchup (page 37) mixed with 2 tablespoons coconut crystals and bake for 45 minutes; let sit for 15 minutes before serving.

Meatloaf Topping

2 Roma tomatoes, seeds removed, diced

I tablespoon coconut crystals

2 teaspoons liquid aminos seasoning

I tablespoon chopped fresh flat-leaf parsley

- Combine all topping ingredients in a small bowl and let sit at room temperature for 15 minutes stirring occasionally.

Eating During Chemotherapy or After Surgery

These bars are a delicious power snack! All seeds and nuts must be quite fresh to avoid mold spores that may attract or feed cancer cells so always check the expiration date on raw nuts and seeds, or freshly hull them yourself. Be sure rolled oats mixture is completely cooled before adding the wet mixture or the chocolate chips will melt.

Magical Moon Energy Bars

2½ cups rolled oats, old-fashioned, uncooked

¼ cup unsweetened coconut flakes

1 cup chopped or slivered raw walnuts, raw macadamia nuts or almonds

½ cup raw sunflower seeds

¾ cup raw pumpkin seeds

2 tablespoons flax seeds

2 tablespoons wheat germ

- Preheat oven to 350°F. Combine all above ingredients in a jelly roll pan (11 x 17), spreading the mixture to the edges of the pan to create a thin layer. Bake for 15-20 minutes, turning once or twice during baking. Transfer mixture to mixing bowl and let cool completely by chilling in refrigerator for 1-2 hours.

While above mixture is cooling, combine the following ingredients in a large bowl:

1 tablespoon ghee, softened

¼ cup EV coconut oil

1 cup coconut nectar

¼ cup unsweetened soy nut butter

1 tablespoon barley malt syrup

2 teaspoons pure vanilla extract

1 teaspoon Ceylon cinnamon

½ teaspoon sea salt

¾ cup bittersweet chocolate chips

- Preheat oven to 350°F. Combine cooled rolled oats mixture with above wet mixture, folding until fully mixed. Spoon into (9x13) baking pan lined with parchment paper (be sure parchment paper extends up over the side of the pan). Press another layer of parchment paper over mixture and apply pressure over entire surface to ensure firmness and provide density to the bars once cooled and cut.

- Remove top layer of parchment paper; bake for 18-20 minutes. Remove from oven and place baking pan on wire rack to cool for 45 minutes. Holding edges of parchment paper; lift granola to cutting surface and let cool for 1 hour before cutting into 1½-inch x 4-inch bars.

- Individually wrap bars in waxed paper and store in refrigerator for up to 2 weeks. Bars may be frozen for up to 3 months if tightly wrapped.

Served over a bed of fresh mixed greens that have been drizzled with EV olive oil and fresh lemon juice, this chicken dish is light and deliciously good for you!

Raspberry Dream Chicken

Serves 4

½ batch Bionic Blueberry Syrup (page 30) but replace blueberries with raspberries
3-4 medium boneless, skinless chicken breasts

Herbes de Provence
Sea salt and freshly ground black pepper
Mixed greens, drizzled with EV olive oil and fresh lemon juice

- Prepare raspberry syrup as directed and set aside.

- Preheat oven to 400°F. Rinse chicken breasts and pat dry. Place them individually between two layers of plastic wrap or into a zip-lock bag not completely sealed to let air escape. Flatten chicken breasts slightly with a mallet (or whatever works, such as a can of tomatoes). Remove from bag, drizzle lightly with EV olive oil and season both sides with Herbes de Provence, sea salt and freshly ground black pepper as desired. Place on parchment-lined baking sheet. Bake for 11-13 minutes. Remove from oven; cover and set aside. Reheat raspberry sauce on low heat.

- Plate the mixed greens (if that's what you are serving with this dish). Place chicken on top of greens and drizzle with raspberry sauce. Serve immediately.

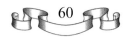

Fuzzy Fish Bake

Serves 2-4

1 pound fresh halibut, salmon or haddock
2 large shredded wheat cereal biscuits
⅓ cup whole spelt flour
1 teaspoon sea salt
1 teaspoon Herbes de Provence
1 teaspoon lemon pepper
¼ teaspoon paprika
½ cup egg wash (2 egg whites with 3 tablespoons water, whisk well)
EV olive oil
Lemon wedges for serving

- Preheat oven to 400°F. De-bone fish and cut into four equal-sized pieces. In a food processor, grind the shredded wheat cereal biscuits to the consistency of bread crumbs. Transfer to a shallow bowl and add the flour, herbs and spices; blend well.

- Pour the egg wash into a separate shallow bowl. Preheat an oven-proof skillet on the stovetop on high heat. Begin coating fish by dipping it into the egg wash, and then rolling it in the flour mixture until it is completely coated; set aside. Repeat with remaining pieces of fish. Pour ¼ cup EV olive oil into the heated pan and immediately place the fish steaks in the pan and brown for 2 minutes. Turn fish steaks over and brown for 1 minute more; place in preheated oven and bake for 9 minutes. Serve immediately with lemon wedges.

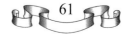

Eating During Chemotherapy or After Surgery

The Rainbow's green goodness shines through in this salad. It offers a giant energy boost.

St. Patty's Day Salad with Shamrock Dressing

Serves 4-6

I bunch fresh baby spinach

2 celery ribs, chopped

Handful of sugar snap peas, de-stringed, cut in half

2 scallions, chopped

½ cup chopped broccoli

2 tablespoons chopped fresh flat-leafed parsley

2 tablespoons chopped fresh cilantro

2-3 tablespoons raw pumpkin seeds

• Rinse and thoroughly dry the vegetables and herbs. Place all ingredients in a salad bowl. Top with Shamrock Dressing, toss and serve.

Shamrock Dressing

¼ cup coconut nectar

¼ teaspoon lime zest

3 tablespoons lime juice

1½ teaspoons poppy seeds

¼ teaspoon sea salt

⅛ teaspoon ground coriander

¼ cup canola oil

• In a deep bowl, place all dressing ingredients except for the canola oil. Whisk briefly, and then slowly add the canola oil while whisking briskly for at least 2 minutes. Pour over salad and enjoy!

Eating During Chemotherapy or After Surgery

Tuna is one of those healthy, oily fishes (along with salmon, trout, halibut and herring) that is loaded with Omega-3 fatty acids, is anti-inflammatory, and boosts our immune systems.

Tuna Boat Salad

Serves 4-6

To Bake Tuna

2 fresh tuna steaks cut in half

¼ cup EV olive oil

Sea salt and freshly ground black pepper

1 medium onion, sliced

1 large clove garlic, sliced

2 tablespoons fresh, flat-leafed parsley

¼ cup water

2 tablespoons lemon juice

- Preheat oven to 350°F. Rub the tuna steaks with EV olive oil and sprinkle with sea salt and pepper. In the bottom of a covered casserole dish, drizzle a little olive oil and place a layer of onions and a few slivers of garlic. Place two of the tuna steaks side by side on top of the layer of onions. Top with a third of the fresh parsley. Repeat with more but not all of the onions, garlic and parsley and with all of the remaining tuna, slightly offset so that both layers cook evenly. Drizzle top with olive oil and sprinkle with remaining parsley, onions and garlic. Pour the water around the sides of the tuna and drizzle with lemon juice; cover and bake for 30 minutes or until center of tuna is a soft pink, or 25 minutes if you prefer you tuna rare.

For Salad

Bibb lettuce leaves, rinsed and dried

2-3 medium tomatoes

10 basil leaves, rinsed and dried, cut into quarters

Red onion slices

Shredded vegetable mozzarella cheese

¼ cup EV olive oil

2-3 tablespoon fresh lemon juice

Sea salt and freshly ground black pepper

- In a shallow salad bowl, assemble lettuce leaves around edge and on bottom of bowl. In a circular pattern starting on the outside of the bowl, place tomato and onion slices until a circle is formed. Flake the slightly cooled tuna steaks with a fork and place half the tuna around the bowl next to the tomatoes in a circular pattern. Repeat with remaining tomatoes, then with remaining tuna until you reach the center of the bowl. Tuck basil leaf quarters randomly between the tomatoes and tuna. Sprinkle with vegetable mozzarella cheese, olive oil and lemon juice. Season to taste with sea salt and black pepper.

Eating During Chemotherapy or After Surgery

Tummy Soothers

Many types of cancer and related chemotherapy drugs can cause nausea, vomiting, diarrhea, and loss of appetite. Sometimes taste preferences change, and sometimes your child won't be able to tolerate the smell or texture of something that has always been a favorite before the cancer and subsequent treatments.

The following recipes, some of them from the Knights of the Magical Moon, contain soothing ingredients that will hopefully comfort your child's upset tummy before, during and after cancer treatment.

Chicken soup boosts our immune system, warms the soul and even soothes an upset stomach when spicy or heavy foods can't be tolerated. Here's a simple yet wholesome and healthy version of a classic comfort food. Serve it with Billowy Biscuits (page 29).

Ginger Chicken Soup with Vegetable Medley

Serves 6

2 tablespoons EV olive oil
I small red onion, halved and thinly sliced
3 cloves garlic, minced
2 tablespoons peeled, grated fresh ginger
2 quarts low-sodium chicken broth
¼ cup chopped turnip
I cup thinly sliced carrots
2 ribs celery, thinly sliced
I teaspoon sea salt
¼ teaspoon freshly ground black pepper
I teaspon fresh (or ¼ teaspoon dried) thyme
½ cup chopped green beans
I (2 to 2½ pound) pre-cooked rotisserie chicken
½ cup frozen peas
4 green onions, sliced
10 ounces multigrain yolkless egg noodles (optional)

- Heat the olive oil in a heavy bottomed stock pot or Dutch oven on medium heat. Add the onion, garlic and ginger; cook, stirring, approximately 3 minutes.

- Add the broth. Stir in the turnip, carrots, celery and seasonings. Bring to a boil, reduce heat and simmer for 15-20 minutes or until vegetables are tender but not too overly done, adding the green beans in the last 5 minutes of cooking. Shred the chicken meat and add it to the pot along with the peas and green onions. Cook until heated through, approximately 5 minutes. If you would like to add noodles, cook separately according to package directions and place in bottom of serving bowls and top with the soup.

This healthy soft drink, full of antioxidants, will help soothe that upset stomach and is very refreshing.

Jammin' Ginger Ale

Makes 4 cups

2½ cups water
¼ cup coconut
   crystals
2-inch piece fresh
   ginger, peeled, cut
   into thirds
2 green (or white)
   tea bags
2 teaspoons lemon juice
2 cups sparkling water

- Place 2½ cups water (not the sparkling water), the coconut crystals and ginger in a saucepan. Bring to a boil; reduce heat and simmer 5 minutes. Remove from heat and add tea bags. Let mixture sit for 5 minutes, covered. Discard tea bags and ginger pieces. Add lemon juice. Chill for a minimum of 2 hours. Add sparkling water and serve in tall glasses over ice.

Broccoli and parsley are rich in Vitamins A & C, calcium, iron and protein!

Michael's Cream of **Broccoli** Soup

Serves 6-8

1 tablespoon ghee

1 medium onion, diced

4 cups low-sodium chicken or vegetable broth

2 heads fresh broccoli with very top of stems, chopped

4 medium potatoes, peeled, diced

1-2 cups soy or rice milk (or enough for desired thickness)

1 teaspoons sea salt

½ teaspoon freshly ground black pepper

- In a large covered saucepan or stock pot, melt the ghee over medium heat; add the diced onion and cook, stirring occasionally until softened, about 8 minutes. Add the broth and vegetables and bring to a boil over high heat. Reduce heat and simmer until vegetables are tender (about 15 minutes). Remove from heat, transfer mixture to a bowl and let it cool for 15 minutes.

- Scoop half the broth and cooked vegetables into a blender. Pulse mixture until creamy, but leaving a few small chunks of vegetables intact for texture. Place pureed mixture back into the stockpot. Scoop the remaining half of the broth and cooked vegetables into blender; pulse until creamy and place back into the stockpot along with the first processed batch. Add soy or rice milk, sea salt and black pepper; heat to a simmer and cook for 5 minutes. Do not allow soup to boil.

- Adjust seasoning to taste. This soup is great with Billowy Biscuits (page 29).

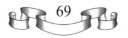

Puffy Popovers with Sweet Lemon Syrup

Makes 5 Popovers

5 egg whites (at room temperature)
I cup soy or rice milk (divided)
½ teaspoon lemon extract
½ cup unbleached, all-purpose flour
½ cup whole wheat flour
¼ teaspoon sea salt
Pinch of baking soda
Soft ghee for greasing tins

- Preheat oven to 450°F. In the bowl of an electric mixer fitted with a whisk attachment, beat the egg whites with ½ cup of the soy or rice milk along with the lemon extract. In a separate bowl, blend the flour with sea salt and baking soda. With mixer on low speed, slowly add flour mixture to milk mixture. When mixed, stop the beater, scrape the sides of the bowl with spatula, turn mixer to medium speed and slowly add the rest of the milk. Beat 2 minutes. Turn to high speed and beat for 5 minutes. Batter should be smooth.

- This recipe makes 5 popovers in popover tins and 8-10 popovers in medium muffin tins. Grease popover or muffin tins generously with melted ghee. If muffin tins are used, fill the end cups only and fill to the top if you want high, large popovers but be sure tops of tins are greased too. If using popover tins, fill to three-quarters full. Bake on middle shelf of oven for 15 minutes. Without opening oven door, reduce heat to 350°F and cook for additional 20 minutes (only 10 minutes if in muffin tins). These are best when served immediately, but may be kept in warm oven with door open for additional 5 minutes if necessary. Serve drizzled with Sweet Lemon Syrup (recipe follows).

Sweet Lemon Syrup

½ cup ghee
2 tablespoons coconut nectar
Juice of ½ lemon

- Place ingredients in small saucepan and heat until ghee is melted and syrup is warm. Drizzle over popovers and enjoy the messy goodness!

Eating During Chemotherapy or After Surgery

Scotty Davidson's Mom says, "During Scotty's second [chemo] protocol he nearly lost his taste for everything. Meals were very hard in our household and he had an aversion to nearly everything - even meat. The only things that he really seemed to like were mashed potatoes and these beans. They are sweet, meatless, and full of fiber. I figured if he was going to eat something sweet at least they were beans and not cake or other goodies. These are truly a "pot of goodness" and got us through this past year. We hope you all enjoy them."

Using barley malt syrup and coconut crystals in place of molasses and brown sugar makes these beans healthier and very tasty.

Scotty D's Baked Beans
(Sir Scotty, The Strong & Serene)

Serves 4-6

1 pound small white dry beans
Water for soaking and parboiling
1 bay leaf
1 medium onion, thinly sliced
3 cups water
1 clove garlic, minced
1 bay leaf
½ teaspoons baking soda
1 teaspoon ground mustard
½ teaspoon ground ginger
1½ teaspoons sea salt
¼ teaspoon freshly ground black pepper
½ cup barley malt syrup
½ cup coconut crystals
3 tablespoons ghee

To Soak and Par-boil Beans

- Soak beans in water for 6-8 hours. Drain beans and place them in a saucepot; add enough water to cover beans. Add bay leaf. Bring to a boil; immediately reduce heat to medium low and let simmer, partially covered, for 15 minutes. Remove bay leaf.

To Cook Beans

- Preheat oven to 300°F. Place half the onion slices in the bottom of the bean pot. Add the beans to the bean pot. In a pan, heat 3 cups of water and add the remaining ingredients except for the remaining onion slices; stir to blend. Pour this mixture over the beans (just enough to cover beans) finishing with water if necessary. Add the remaining onion slices. Cover and bake for 6-7 hours or until beans are tender, adding water occasionally if necessary; again just to cover beans. Serve with Kool Ketchup (page 37) if desired.

Sorbets usually require an ice cream machine but by whipping the egg white and stirring the mixture during the first few hours of freezing, the consistency is very sorbet-like. Try using kiwi fruit, raspberries or blueberries to make similar, wonderfully refreshing sorbets!

Smashing Strawberry Sorbet

Serves 4

½ cup coconut crystals
¼ cup cooled green tea or sparkling water
4 cups fresh strawberries, hulled
  and cleaned

1 teaspoon
  fresh lemon juice
1 egg white, whipped

- In a medium saucepan, combine the coconut crystals and green tea or sparkling water. Cook over medium heat, stirring until crystals are dissolved. Set aside to cool completely.

- In a blender or food processor, puree the strawberries. (Two cups of puree needed.) Strain through a fine-meshed sieve for a silky sorbet. Add the lemon juice to the strawberry puree. Stir the strawberry puree into the cooled green tea mixture and refrigerate for 2 hours, covered.

- Whip the egg white until soft peaks form. Fold into the strawberry mixture, cover and freeze for 1 hour. Remove from freezer and briskly stir the mixture. Re-cover and freeze for 30 minutes longer. Stir again, re-cover and freeze for 1 more hour. It's ready to serve!

Lexie says that mashed potatoes are her ultimate tummy soother during and after chemotherapy. Adding sweet potatoes makes it even better by adding loads of Vitamins A & C and needed carbohydrates. Sweet potatoes also contain lutein and carotenoids, molecules shown to starve cancer cells. Keeping the potato skin on while steaming the Yukon Gold potatoes will retain some of the potato's essential nutrients. While most of the nutrients are in the potato, the skin is a great source of natural fiber. The skin also contains iron, protein and natural sweetness.

Soothing Smashed Potatoes

Serves 6-8

2 medium sweet potatoes
3 medium Yukon Gold potatoes, quartered
2 cloves garlic, peeled, whole
½ cup rice or soy milk
¼ cup low-sodium chicken broth

3 tablespoons ghee
½ teaspoon sea salt
½ teaspoon freshly ground black pepper
Chopped green onions for topping

- Roast sweet potatoes in a preheated 400°F oven for 1 hour or until easily pierced with fork and pulp is soft. Remove from oven and allow potatoes to cool enough to handle. Remove and mash pulp, cover and set aside. Discard peeling.

- Wash and remove blemishes from peeling on Yukon Gold potatoes. Fill bottom half of steamer pan with water. Place quartered potatoes in top half of covered steamer pan with the whole peeled cloves of garlic. Bring to a boil, reduce heat and steam on medium high until potatoes are very soft when pierced with a fork (about 30 minutes, checking off and on to be sure water has not boiled away during steaming process). Remove potatoes and garlic from steamer, mash and combine with sweet potatoes in a medium bowl.

- Place rice or soy milk, chicken broth and ghee into a small saucepan and heat until ghee is mostly melted and mixture is warm. Stir the milk mixture, sea salt and black pepper into the mashed potatoes a little at a time to desired consistency. Using an electric mixer beat the potatoes until light and fluffy. Sprinkle with chopped green onions to serve.

Eating During Chemotherapy or After Surgery

Just for FUN!

Laughter is the best medicine! While more research must be done, it is believed by many that laughter, along with a positive attitude, helps boost our immune systems, makes us breathe faster (and that helps to send more oxygen to our tissues), lowers blood sugar levels, aids in proper blood flow, and opens our hearts to more of the good things in life.

Lexie and her Mom, Alice, during "The Blender Incident" at our first cooking event at the Friendship House in Norwell, MA

At the Magical Moon Farm in the center of The Garden of Hope there is a crescent-shaped patch of organically grown blueberry bushes where the knights can pick berries that haven't been sprayed with chemicals. During the summer, the knights create artwork with Donna Green in the arbor right next to this wonderful Blueberry Crescent Moon.

Blueberry Crescent Moons (Breakfast Cookies)

Makes 12-15 Crescent Moons

¾ cup quinoa flakes

¾ cup white rice flour

½ cup tapioca flour

5 tablespoons potato starch

¼ cup unsweetened shredded coconut

1 teaspoon baking powder (cornstarch-free)

1 teaspoon baking soda

¼ teaspoon xanthan gum

½ teaspoon guar gum

½ teaspoon ground Ceylon cinnamon

½ cup coconut nectar

½ teaspoon lemon extract

¼ cup canola oil

1 egg white

Fresh blueberries

- Preheat oven to 325°F. Line a cookie sheet with parchment paper.

- In a mixing bowl, combine dry ingredients and blend gently with spoon. Add coconut nectar, lemon extract, canola oil, and egg white. Stir well (do not mix with electric mixer).

- Roll dough on lightly floured (rice flour) board and flatten to ¼ inch thick. Shape with crescent cookie cutter, reusing/re-rolling dough with as little flour as possible (or using two tablespoons dough at a time, shaped by hand). Place each crescent onto parchment lined baking sheet. Top each crescent with 4-6 fresh blueberries, and sprinkle with a little cinnamon. Bake for 12 minutes or until golden. Place crescents on wire rack to cool.

I Scream Ice Cream

Makes 2 cups

⅓ cup coconut nectar

⅛ teaspoon baking soda (scant)

3 egg whites

1½ teaspoons pure vanilla extract

⅓ cup vanilla soy milk

½ cup silken vanilla tofu

1 tablespoon ghee

⅓ cup bittersweet chocolate chips

- Whisk first 5 ingredients together in a small saucepan; heat on medium low until thickened slightly, stirring with a wooden spoon. Add the tofu and ghee and stir. The tofu will break up into small pieces but will not melt completely. Do not allow mixture to boil. After cooking 10 minutes, remove from heat and put mixture through a fine strainer into the saucepan, pushing the softened tofu bits down through the strainer to break them up. Set burner to medium and simmer mixture for 5 minutes. Remove from heat and add chocolate chips. Stir to melt.

- Cover and place in refrigerator for 2 hours. Transfer ice cream to plastic freezer container with cover (or popsicle molds) and freeze for a minimum of 2 hours before serving.

This super tasty, super crispy snack is fun to eat and so healthy - full of protein, thiamin, riboflavin, folate, iron and magnesium, and is a very good source of dietary fiber, Vitamins A, C, B6 and E, calcium, potassium, copper and manganese. Kale is a top-scoring antioxidant vegetable!

Krispy **Kale** Chips

Serves 4-6

1 large bunch fresh kale
EV olive oil
¼ teaspoon sea salt
Granulated garlic

- Preheat oven to 350°F. Remove kale leaves from stem; rinse and thoroughly dry leaves (important). Fold leaves in half at the spine, with underside exposed. Cut away majority of tough spine with scissors.

- Lay leaves on large parchment or foil-lined baking pan and drizzle with EV olive oil. Gently rub both sides of leaves with the oil until coated. Sprinkle lightly with sea salt and granulated garlic. Bake for 7 minutes; gently turn leaves over and bake for 5 more minutes or until leaves are crispy and edges are slightly browned. Gently remove from pan and serve immediately or within a few hours.

"When I was going through treatment my mom made this for me all the time. I had to take some oral chemo at home and it was yucky! I love lemons! So here's how she made it. Sometimes I help juice the lemons."

– Michael Lanosa
(Sir Michael, Knight of the Magical Sun)

We substituted sugar with the juice of steamed apples and a touch of coconut nectar to lower the glycemic index in Michael's delicious lemonade.

Michael's Sunshine Lemonade

Makes 1 quart

2 red apples of choice, rinsed, quartered, cored (keep skin on)
2 cups distilled water for bottom of steamer pot
1 tablespoon coconut nectar
2 cups distilled water
Juice of 2-3 lemons (to taste)
Lemon slices for serving

- Place the cored, quartered apples in the top of a steamer. Place 2 cups of distilled water in the bottom section of the pot. Steam the apples for 20 minutes over medium high heat.

- Combine the steamed apples with the steamer water and mash with a potato masher. Over a 4-quart bowl, pour this mixture into a fine mesh sieve. Push pulp against the sieve with the back of a spoon to get all the juices. Discard pulp and peel. You should have 1½ cups apple juice. Immediately add the coconut nectar to the warmed apple juice and stir to dissolve; chill for 1 hour. Add the additional 2 cups distilled water and fresh lemon juice, stir. Serve over crushed ice and garnished with lemon slices.

These chocolate bundles of sweet and salty goodness are a great way to reward your child with a treat; and they're super easy to make!

Noble Knight Nougats

Makes 15 nougats

I (10-ounce) bag bittersweet chocolate chips

I tablespoon EV coconut oil

¼ cup unsweetened coconut flakes

½ cup raw unsalted pumpkin seeds

I cup chopped raw unsalted macadamia nuts

½ teaspoon coarse sea salt

- Place 14-16 mini paper cupcake liners in mini cupcake tin.

- Place water in the bottom of a double boiler. Place chocolate chips in top of double boiler. Once water has boiled, reduce heat to medium high and when chips begin to melt, add the EV coconut oil. Just as soon as mixture is melted, remove from heat and add remaining ingredients and stir.

- With a spoon or very small ice cream scoop, fill each lined mini cupcake tin (heaping). Chill for 30 minutes; remove nougats from tin and wrap individually in plastic wrap. Store in refrigerator, or if you like them softer, set out at room temperature for 1 hour before eating.

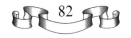

It's fun to split the bag open at the table (carefully parents - to avoid steam burns)!

Potatoes in a Bag

Serves 4-6

A few red, purple or yellow potatoes of your choice, with skin on, and cubed (2-inch)
1 large sweet potato, peeled and cubed (2-inch)
2 tablespoons EV olive oil
1 tablespoon chopped fresh flat-leafed parsley
1 teaspoon chopped fresh thyme
2 teaspoons chopped fresh rosemary
1 teaspoon sea salt

- Preheat oven to 375°F. In a medium bowl, toss the potatoes with the oil, using your hands. Sprinkle the potatoes with the herbs and sea salt and toss again. Transfer the potatoes to a sheet of parchment paper large enough to enclose them. Fold the paper loosely 3 or 4 times on the ends and at the top to seal. If necessary, divide the potatoes into two or three separate "parchment bags" in order to get them to fold and seal. Place bags on a cookie sheet. Bake for 1 hour. Serve immediately.

Pudding It Nicely

Serves 6

2 cups (12 ounces) bittersweet chocolate chips
⅓ cup coconut crystals
½ teaspoon sea salt
1½ cups soy or rice milk
¼ cup ghee

• Place chocolate chips and coconut crystals in a blender; cover and process until chips are coarsely chopped. Add the sea salt.

• In a saucepan over medium to medium high heat, bring soy or rice milk and ghee to a boil. Add to blender; cover and process until chips are melted and mixture is smooth (it won't take long). Pour into six individual serving dishes.

These little treats brighten up any dish!

Rainbow Shish Kebabs

On a thick long toothpick or wooden skewer, place the following slices of fruit/whole berries in this order: black or red grape, blueberry, kiwi fruit, banana, orange, and raspberry or strawberry and serve it by itself or with many of the recipes featured in this cookbook.

Gluten-Free is for Me

Wild varieties of fresh or frozen blueberries (such as Wyman's® of Maine brand) show the greatest amount of antioxidant activity, and the flavor is more intense.

Royal Blueberry Muffins

Makes 12 medium or 6-8 large muffins

4 egg whites
1 cup soy or rice milk
½ teaspoon lemon extract
¾ cup canola oil
2 cups plus 2 tablespoons gluten-free all-purpose baking flour (such as Bob's Red Mill® brand)
½ cup tapioca flour
¼ teaspoon xanthan gum
½ teaspoon guar gum
½ cup plus 2 tablespoons coconut crystals
4 teaspoons baking powder (cornstarch-free)
1 teaspoon sea salt
1 cup fresh or frozen blueberries coated with 2 teaspoons tapioca flour
Ceylon cinnamon for topping

- Preheat oven to 415°F. In a mixing bowl, combine egg whites and other liquid ingredients. In a separate bowl, blend flours and xanthan/guar gum with coconut crystals until there are no lumps. Add baking powder and sea salt to dry mixture. Add dry mixture to liquid mixture and blend by hand just until smooth. Fold in blueberries.

- Line muffin tins with paper cups and fill with batter to three quarters full. Sprinkle top with Ceylon cinnamon. Bake for 18-20 minutes.

Chocolate Chip Bundt Cake

Serves 6-8

½ cup gluten-free all purpose baking flour such as Bob's Red Mill® brand (blend of potato, sorghum, tapioca, garbanzo and fava bean flours)

¼ cup rice flour

½ cup tapioca flour

¼ teaspoon xanthan gum

¼ teaspoon guar gum

½ cup cocoa

1½ teaspoons baking soda

¾ teaspoon baking powder (cornstarch-free)

½ teaspoon sea salt

1⅓ cups coconut crystals

⅓ cup canola oil

1½ tablespoons melted ghee

4 egg whites

1 teaspoon pure vanilla extract

1 cup soy or rice milk with 1 tablespoon lemon juice

¾ cup bittersweet chocolate chips

EV coconut oil and rice flour to coat pan

Fresh raspberries or unsweetened coconut flakes for topping

- Preheat oven to 325°F. Combine the dry ingredients in a small bowl. In a large mixing bowl, beat the oil, ghee, egg whites, and vanilla extract. Add the dry ingredients and soy or rice milk (w/lemon juice) alternately, starting and ending with the dry ingredients. Stir in the chocolate chips.

- Pour the batter into a Bundt pan that has been greased with EV coconut oil and floured with all-purpose gluten-free flour. Bake for 40-45 minutes. Cool in the pan for 10 minutes before inverting onto a platter. Top with unsweetened coconut flakes or serve with fresh raspberries.

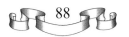

Gluten-Free is for Me

Cuckoo for Coconut Tea Bread

Makes 1 loaf

For Bread

1½ cups plus 1 tablespoon gluten-free all purpose flour mix (such as Bob's Red Mill® brand)

¾ cup coconut crystals

1½ teaspoons xanthan gum

1 tablespoon baking powder (cornstarch-free)

¼ teaspoon sea salt

1 tablespoon chia seeds

Grated zest of 1 medium orange

¾ cup shredded unsweetened coconut

¾ cup light coconut milk

2 tablespoons canola oil

2 tablespoons coconut oil, melted and slightly cooled

4 egg whites

Freshly squeezed juice from 1 medium orange (reserve 2 tablespoons for glaze)

For Glaze

½ cup coconut nectar

2 tablespoons freshly squeezed orange juice

- Whisk glaze ingredients together and set aside.

- Grease one (8 x 4) loaf pan generously with ghee or coconut oil or line with parchment paper.

- Mix gluten-free all purpose flour, coconut crystals, xanthan gum, baking powder, sea salt, chia seeds, orange zest and shredded coconut in a large bowl. Use a whisk to thoroughly combine these dry ingredients.

- In a separate bowl whisk together coconut milk, canola oil, coconut oil, egg whites and orange juice until well blended. Stir the liquid ingredients into the dry ingredients and mix just until blended. Using a rubber spatula, transfer the batter to the loaf pan. Let the bread sit uncovered for about 30 minutes. While bread batter is resting, preheat oven to 350°F. Prepare the glaze by whisking the coconut crystals and freshly squeezed orange juice in a small bowl, until smooth. Set aside.

- Bake for 50-55 minutes or until a toothpick inserted in the middle of the loaf comes out clean. Set the loaf pan on a cooling rack and using a wooden skewer or toothpick, poke about 24 holes in the top of loaf. Spoon the glaze over the top of the loaf and allow the loaf to cool in the pan for about 30 minutes. Remove loaf from pan; cut when completely cooled.

Gluten-Free is for Me

Substitute 2 cups of gluten-free, all-purpose baking flour such as Bob's Red Mill® brand for the tapioca and brown rice flour if desired. These types of pre-packaged mixed gluten-free flours often contain a mixture of garbanzo bean flour, potato starch, tapioca flour, white sorghum flour and fava bean flour. Parchment paper should be used, as gluten-free dough tends to stick to the baking sheet.

Imperial Biscuits (Gluten-free)

Makes 8-9 biscuits

1 cup tapioca flour

1 cup brown rice flour

¼ teaspoon xanthan gum

½ teaspoon guar gum

4 teaspoons baking powder (cornstarch-free)

½ teaspoon baking soda

1 teaspoon sea salt

¼ cup cold ghee, cut into small cubes

¾ cup plus one tablespoon rice or soy milk with 1 tablespoon fresh lemon juice

2 egg whites, slightly beaten

- Preheat oven to 425°F. Line one large baking sheet with parchment paper. In a medium bowl, combine dry ingredients lightly with a fork. Add the chilled ghee cubes and work into the dry ingredients with a pastry cutter or with your fingers until the mixture feels granular and the ghee is the size of small peas.

- In a measuring cup place the rice or soy milk and lemon. Let this mixture sit for 10 minutes. Add the egg whites. Pour the wet ingredients into the flour mixture and mix with a spoon or fork until just combined.

- Drop by ice cream scoop onto the parchment-lined baking sheet. (This is a wet and sticky batter so the ease of a drop biscuit works well for this recipe.) Immediately lower oven temperature to 400°F; bake biscuits for 15-18 minutes or until bottoms are golden brown. Transfer hot biscuits to cooling rack. Serve warm or cold.

Gluten-Free is for Me

Always use parchment paper for gluten-free cookies to keep them from sticking to the baking sheet.

Gluten-Free Gingersnaps

Makes 24 cookies

¾ cup ghee, softened

1 cup plus 2 tablespoons coconut crystals

¼ cup barley malt syrup

2 egg whites

2 cups gluten-free, all-purpose baking flour (such as Bob's Red Mill® brand)

¼ teaspoon xanthan gum

¼ teaspoon guar gum

½ teaspoon baking soda

½ teaspoon sea salt

1½ teaspoons ground ginger

1 teaspoon ground Ceylon cinnamon

½ teaspoon ground cloves

- Preheat oven to 350°F. Using a wooden spoon, cream ghee, coconut crystals and barley malt syrup until blended. Add egg whites and blend until smooth, again by hand. In a separate bowl, combine dry ingredients and add to creamed mixture. Stir until well blended.

- Drop by small ice cream scoop or heaping tablespoon onto baking sheet lined with parchment paper (cookies will expand so allow 3 inches between cookies). Bake for 14-16 minutes. Transfer cookies to cooling rack immediately and allow cookies to cool completely before serving.

This recipe is great served with Awesome Oven Fries (page 103).

Hold-the-Bun Burgers with Fresh Basil Pesto

Makes 4 burgers

I pound ground grass-fed bison
I teaspoon Montreal Steak Seasoning (recipe follows)
4 large Bibb or Butter lettuce leaves, rinsed and dried
Fresh basil pesto (page 33)
I fresh tomato, thinly sliced
Red onion, thinly sliced

- Using your hands or a fork, blend the ground bison with the Montreal Steak Seasoning. Form into four burgers. Grill or broil to desired doneness.

- Center each burger on one large lettuce leaf; top with basil pesto, fresh tomato and onion slices. Wrap lettuce leaf around burger and secure lettuce in place with toothpick. Serve warm.

Montreal Steak Seasoning
2 teaspoons garlic powder
4 teaspoons coarsely ground coriander seed
2 tablespoons coarse sea salt
I tablespoon dried dill weed
I tablespoon plus I teaspoon paprika
I tablespoon red pepper flakes
I tablespoon plus I teaspoon freshly ground black pepper

- Combine all ingredients and store in airtight container.

Salmon Skewers with Squished Potatoes and Broccoli

Serves 4

1½ pounds baby red potatoes

Coarse sea salt

1 bunch fresh broccoli, chopped

½ pound fresh skinless salmon fillet, cut into 1-inch cubes

1 small red or yellow onion, peel off layers

2 tablespoons EV olive oil

Sea salt

Lemon pepper

Fresh or dried dill weed

2 tablespoons coconut nectar

Fresh lemon juice

2 tablespoons trans fat free buttery spread

Lemon wedges for serving

- Preheat broiler. In a medium steamer pot, steam potatoes sprinkled with coarse sea salt until fork tender – about 15 minutes. Set aside but keep covered. Steam the chopped broccoli for 3 minutes. Remove from heat but keep covered.

- With oven rack in center of oven, heat broiler on high heat. Thread pieces of salmon alternately with pieces of red or yellow onion layers onto skewers. Place skewers in a single layer on broiler pan and drizzle with EV olive oil and season with sea salt, lemon pepper and dill weed. If skewers are wooden, fold aluminum foil over exposed ends to prevent burning. Broil salmon until opaque throughout; approximately 8 minutes (flipping once after 4 minutes). Remove from oven and while hot, drizzle with coconut nectar and fresh lemon juice.

- Drain potatoes. While they are still hot, press on them with the back of a tablespoon so they are slightly "squished". Plate the potatoes and top with buttery spread. Plate the salmon skewers and broccoli along with a wedge of lemon and serve immediately.

Salmon is filled with necessary Omega 3 fatty acids, protein, selenium (antioxidant) and Vitamins A, B6 & B12. You will need 4 skewers for this recipe.

Set the table with chopsticks for this tasty dish!

Skinny Noodles Stir Fry

Serves 6

8 ounces thin rice noodles

⅔ cup low-sodium chicken broth, warmed

1 teaspoon toasted sesame oil

2 tablespoons liquid aminos seasoning

3 tablespoons chopped green onions

Freshly ground black pepper to taste

⅛ teaspoon red pepper flakes

Canola oil for stir frying

2 cloves garlic, peeled and thinly sliced

2 cups chopped fresh bok choy, Swiss chard, or greens of choice

1 cup chopped fresh broccoli

Handful of snow peas

2 tablespoons chopped fresh mint for topping

- Cook rice noodles according to package directions but reduce cooking time by 1 minute. Drain noodles and set aside. In a small bowl, whisk together warm chicken broth, sesame oil, liquid aminos seasoning, chopped green onions, black pepper and red pepper flakes. Set aside.

- Heat a wok or heavy-bottomed large sauté pan. Add 2 table-spoons canola oil, the garlic, greens, broccoli and snow peas. Stir fry for 3 minutes, lifting and turning vegetables often with two wooden spatulas or spoons. Add the noodles and the chicken broth mixture and lift and turn all ingredients gently for 30 seconds to blend flavors and re-heat the noodles.

- Remove from heat and transfer everything to a platter. Top with chopped mint. Serve immediately.

Bewitching Brownies

Makes 9 thick gluten-free brownies

5 egg whites

I cup coconut nectar

I teaspoon pure vanilla extract

½ cup ghee, melted

¼ cup canola oil

1½ cups fine rice flour or chickpea
   (garbanzo) flour or gluten-free flour blend
   (all-purpose, such as Bob's Red Mill® brand)

½ teaspoon baking powder (cornstarch-free)

¼ teaspoon xanthan gum

¼ teaspoon guar gum

½ cup baking cocoa

½ teaspoon sea salt

¾ cup bittersweet chocolate chips

½ cup chopped raw macadamia nuts or
   walnuts

• Preheat oven to 350°F. Line a (9 x 9) baking pan with parchment paper.

• Mix all wet ingredients with a wooden spoon in a large bowl until well blended. Combine dry ingredients and add to wet mixture, again stirring by hand. Fold in chocolate chips and macadamia nuts or walnuts. Pour into prepared pan and bake 22-25 minutes.

• Allow to cool in pan on wire rack for 20 minutes. Holding sides of parchment paper, lift brownies out of pan. Cut into squares once cooled.

Healthy Equals Tasty

Nutritionists tell us to eat a wide variety of foods every day. This helps us to get all the nutrients our bodies need to maintain good health. Proteins, fats, carbohydrates, vitamins, minerals and trace minerals are all important to achieving a balanced diet.

Other important substances in powerhouse vegetables, fruits, beans and whole grains are called phytochemicals, also known as phytonutrients, and they come solely from plants. Phytochemicals are an important buffer against cancer development and contain many cancer-fighting compounds with strange names like antioxidants, carnosols, flavonoids, flavones, isoflavones, catechins, anthocyanins, isothiocyanates, carotenoids, allyl sulfides, and polyphenols.

It is important (and fun, and empowering!) to research the phytochemical types/qualities in each plant food that you eat to learn what individual strengths they have to help stave away carcinogens. For instance, carotenoids have potent antioxidant properties and are found in mostly orange-colored foods such as carrots, sweet potatoes, and winter squash. Allyl sulfides are in bulb vegetables such as onions, leeks, garlic, shallots and chives while isothiocyanates are another sulfur-based compound found in broccoli, cabbage, watercress, turnip and radish and they all work hard against toxic chemicals that try to invade our bodies. Flavenoids are in cucumbers, squash, tomatoes, eggplant, broccoli, cabbage, berries and citrus fruits. They block various stages of carcinogen growth. Curcumin stave away destructive oxygen radicals and are in turmeric and mustard.

Be adventurous! Eat new organic vegetables, grains, berries and fruits that you've never tried before and learn about how they help you to stay strong.

Potatoes contain carbohydrates, necessary for weight gain during cancer treatment. Try to cook these fries in a single layer or only slightly overlapping if you want them crispy. If you prefer your fries with ketchup, be sure to have some safe and delicious Kool Ketchup all made and ready (page 37).

Awesome Oven Fries

Serves 4

3 tablespoons EV olive oil

4 medium Russet potatoes, skins on

3 cloves garlic, peeled and sliced

1 tablespoon chopped fresh rosemary

1 teaspoon sea salt

⅛ teaspoon freshly ground black pepper

- Preheat oven to 450°F. Sprinkle the EV olive oil in a heavy baking dish. Cut the potatoes into wedges (about 8-10 per potato). Place in baking dish. Add the garlic and sprinkle the chopped rosemary, sea salt and black pepper over the potatoes.

- With your hands, mix all ingredients well, coating the potatoes with the EV olive oil. Roast uncovered for 30 minutes. Turn potatoes with a spatula and roast for another 25-30 minutes. Serve immediately.

Big Ole Biscuit Burgers

Makes 4 Burgers

1 pound ground grass-fed bison
1 teaspoon sea salt
½ teaspoon freshly ground black pepper
½ teaspoon granulated garlic
¼ teaspoon paprika
1 teaspoon liquid aminos seasoning

4 (4-inch diameter) cold Billowy Biscuits (page 29) rolled a little flatter for this recipe.

Dressings and Condiments
Lettuce
Tomato slices
Red onion slices
Vegetable pepper jack or Swiss cheese slices
Mustard (vinegar-free such as Coleman's®)
Kool Ketchup (page 37)

- In a medium bowl, combine the ground bison, spices and seasonings. Form into four burger patties (4-inch diameter); they will shrink slightly. Preheat skillet on medium high heat. Cook burgers on ungreased skillet for 4 minutes; turn and cook for 4 more minutes. Heat biscuits slightly and cut in half horizontally; dress as desired.

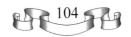

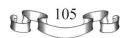

Healthy Equals Tasty

By grinding (or having your butcher grind) boneless, skinless chicken thighs, you end up with a moist and tasty sausage and it ensures that you are not getting chicken byproducts. To save time, trim and grind the chicken thighs the night before cooking.

Breakfast Sausage Patties with Spinach Omelet

Serves 4-6

Breakfast Sausage Patties

2 tablespoons EV olive oil

½ cup finely chopped onion

½ cup finely chopped apple (peeled)

I teaspoon minced garlic

1¾ pounds ground boneless, skinless chicken thighs, trimmed of fat

I tablespoon finely chopped fresh (or one teaspoon dried) thyme

I tablespoon chopped fresh (or one teaspoon dried) sage

½ teaspoon fennel seed, slightly ground

¾ teaspoon sea salt

½ teaspoon freshly ground black pepper

- In a large skillet, heat 2 tablespoons canola oil over medium-high heat. Add the chopped onion and apple; cook, stirring, for 3 to 4 minutes. Add the garlic and cook for 30 seconds. Remove from pan and cool completely. In a large bowl combine the ground chicken, thyme, sage, fennel seed, salt and pepper. Add the cooled onion mixture and mix well. On a flat surface covered with wax paper or aluminum foil, form the mixture into 8 (4-ounce) patties, each about 3 inches in diameter. Heat 2 tablespoons EV olive oil in the same skillet over medium-high heat. Add patties to the pan and cook until golden brown and no longer pink in the middle, 4-5 minutes per side. Remove from the pan and keep warm until ready to serve. Continue using this skillet for the omelet.

Spinach Omelet

2 tablespoons EV olive oil

2 tablespoons finely chopped sweet onion

1½ cups chopped fresh or ¾ cup frozen spinach, thawed and squeezed dry

8-10 egg whites

2-3 slices vegetable pepper jack or Swiss cheese

¼ teaspoon sea salt

⅛ teaspoon freshly ground black pepper

- In the same skillet as was used to cook the sausages, heat the olive oil on medium heat. Add the onion and sauté for 3 minutes. Add the spinach and sauté for another 3 minutes. Add the egg whites, pepper jack or Swiss cheese broken into small pieces, sea salt and black pepper. Cook on one side. Turn heat to low, fold omelet in half carefully with spatula and cook for 1 minute. Flip omelet gently and continue cooking until the egg is cooked through and cheese is slightly melted. Serve immediately with Breakfast Sausage Patties.

Bunny Greens & Fresh Pear Salad

Serves 6

1 head Romaine lettuce

1 bunch arugula or watercress

2 green onions, chopped

6 radishes, sliced

⅓ cup shredded carrot

1 cup diced European cucumber

1 Anjou or Bartlett pear, cored and sliced

2 tablespoons hulled sunflower seeds

- Place all salad ingredients except for the sunflower seeds in a salad bowl or platter. Drizzle with dressing; sprinkle sunflower seeds on top and serve.

Citrus Dressing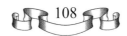

⅓ cup canola oil

1 tablespoon fresh lemon juice

1 tablespoon fresh orange juice

1 teaspoon liquid aminos seasoning

1 teaspoon hot sauce

2 teaspoons coconut nectar or crystals

1 teaspoon sea salt

- Combine all ingredients in a bowl and whisk briskly until well blended.

Olympic Chicken Thighs

Serves 4-6

2 pounds boneless, skinless chicken thighs, rinsed, dried and trimmed of fat.

- Place prepared chicken thighs in a non-reactive bowl or zip-lock bag.

Greek Marinade

½ cup EV olive oil

2½ tablespoons fresh lemon juice

I large clove garlic, minced

1½ teaspoons ground mustard

I tablespoon coconut nectar

I tablespoon chopped fresh (or I teaspoon dried) oregano

½ tablespoon fresh (or ½ teaspoon dried) thyme

I tablespoon chopped fresh (or I teaspoon dried) flat-leafed parsley

2 teaspoons chopped fresh (or ½ teaspoon dried) rosemary

⅛ teaspoon chili pepper flakes (optional)

Sea salt and freshly ground black pepper to taste

- Mix all marinade ingredients and pour over chicken breasts; seal and refrigerate for 2-6 hours.

- Grill chicken thighs on medium low heat, 7 minutes per side, or preheat large cast iron griddle or skillet on stovetop and sear chicken on both sides (1 minute per side). Place skillet with chicken in preheated 400°F oven and bake for approximately 10 minutes or until no longer pink in the center. Serve warm with your favorite salad.

Popeye Salad

Serves 4-6

1½ cups water or low sodium vegetable broth

½ teaspoon sea salt

⅛ teaspoon freshly ground black pepper

1 cup couscous

4 scallions, thinly sliced

2 tablespoons EV olive oil

2 tablespoons lemon juice

3 cups baby spinach

¾ cup fresh basil leaves, roughly chopped

½ cup pine nuts

- In a covered saucepan, bring 1½ cups water or vegetable broth to a boil; season with sea salt and black pepper. Turn off heat and stir in couscous and scallions; toss gently to combine. Cover and let sit for 5 minutes. Add EV olive oil and lemon juice. Gently fold in spinach, chopped basil and pine nuts. Place mixture in a large serving dish. Season to taste and serve at room temperature or chilled.

Sesame Chicken Tenders

Serves 2-3

2 boneless, skinless
   chicken breasts
2 cloves garlic, peeled
   & chopped
½ teaspoon curry
   powder
¼ teaspoon freshly
   ground black pepper
2 tablespoons
   coconut nectar
2 tablespoons
   sesame seed
½ teaspoon sea salt
Sprinkle of red pepper flakes (optional)
2 tablespoons EV olive oil

- Rinse and pat dry chicken breasts. Cut chicken into 2-inch cubes. Add chopped garlic and sprinkle with curry powder and black pepper. Stir to coat chicken pieces evenly and set aside.

- Combine coconut nectar with sesame seeds, sea salt and red pepper flakes (optional); stir to combine. Set aside.

- Preheat heavy-bottomed skillet or wok on medium high to high heat. Add EV olive oil, chicken pieces and garlic. Stir fry chicken for 2-3 minutes turning often until almost cooked through. Add coconut nectar/sesame seed mixture (may need to use rubber spatula to get all that sticky goodness out of the bowl). Stir and turn briskly and stir fry until sesame seeds are slightly toasted and some of coconut nectar has evaporated (about 2 minutes).

- Remove from heat and serve warm with your favorite vegetable or salad.

Sloppy Joe Baked Potatoes

Serves 4

4 medium baking potatoes (Russets work well here)
2 tablespoons EV olive oil
Sea salt and freshly ground black pepper

For Sloppy Joe Mixture
¾ cup chopped yellow onion
½ cup chopped green, red, or orange bell pepper
2 jalapeño peppers, seeded and finely chopped (optional)
2 cloves garlic, minced
I pound ground grass-fed bison or ground turkey

I (14.5-ounce) can diced tomatoes with their juices or 1½ cups fresh diced tomatoes
¼ cup tomato paste
3 tablespoons mustard (vinegar-free such as Coleman's®)
I tablespoon chili powder
1½ teaspoons ground cumin
I teaspoon sea salt
½ teaspoon freshly ground black pepper

• Preheat oven to 400°F. Wash potatoes and pat dry. Place potatoes on a foil-lined baking pan and coat with EV olive oil, sea salt and freshly ground black pepper. Bake 45 minutes to an hour or until potatoes are tender.

• Meanwhile, in a heavy skillet, sauté the onions and bell peppers in the olive oil until soft, approximately 10 minutes. Add the jalapeños and garlic and sauté another 5 minutes. Add the ground meat and cook until browned, stirring and breaking it up with a wooden spoon until meat is crumbled. Add remaining ingredients and simmer for 15 minutes.

• Remove potatoes from oven and using a fork, puncture the top of the potatoes in the form of a cross pattern. Using a towel so you don't burn your hands, squeeze sides of potatoes so that they pop open. Top with ghee and spoon Sloppy Joe mixture onto prepared potatoes and serve with your favorite vegetable side dish.

Pasta Sir Lexie's favorite

This easy one-dish meal offers a lot of goodness and cooks up quickly on those busy days.

Busy Day Pasta

Serves 4-6

½ pound multigrain, low glycemic or gluten-free elbow macaroni
3 tablespoons EV olive oil
6 pre-cooked all natural chicken sausage of choice, sliced into medallions
I red bell pepper, chopped
I medium onion, chopped
2 cloves garlic, minced
I teaspoon sea salt
½ teaspoon freshly ground black pepper
I (28-ounce) can diced tomatoes, with juices
2 teaspoons chopped fresh (or ½ teaspoon dried) oregano
I tablespoon trans fat free buttery spread or ghee
Chopped fresh green onions for topping

- Place olive oil in large skillet and place over high heat. Add sausage, red bell pepper, onion, garlic and spices; immediately reduce to medium heat and simmer for 15 minutes being careful not to burn onions. Add the tomatoes and the oregano and simmer another 10 minutes. Keep warm.

- Meanwhile, boil the pasta according to package directions (al dente). Drain pasta and pour into the skillet with the sausage and tomatoes. Add buttery spread or ghee; stir and top with chopped green onions. Serve immediately.

Dragon's Egg Soup

Serves 6-8

For Breadcrumbs

- Preheat oven to 350°F. Place 2-3 cups of small-cubed Irish Soda Bread (page 35) or other yeast-free bread cubes on parchment or foil-lined baking pan. Sprinkle cubed bread with 2 tablespoons EV olive oil and 1 heaping teaspoon dried Herbes de Provence. Turn with hands to meld oil and herbs; bake for 10 minutes. Turn with spatula and bake 5-7 more minutes or until crisp. Remove from oven and set aside to cool. When cooled, grind into bread crumbs and reserve ¾ cup of crumbs for this recipe.

Dragon's Egg Soup, continued

For the Dragon's Eggs

¾ cup yeast-free bread crumbs

2 teaspoons dried Herbes de Provence

1 teaspoon fresh (or ¼ teaspoon dried) thyme

1 pound ground turkey

2-3 cloves garlic, minced

3 egg whites

¼ cup EV olive oil

2 tablespoons rice or soy milk

1 teaspoon sea salt

½ teaspoon freshly ground black pepper

⅔ cup frozen peas

- Preheat oven to 400°F. Place Dragon's Egg ingredients (except for green peas) in bowl and mix with hands just until blended. Add the peas and fold in gently. Form into balls 1½ inches in diameter and place on baking sheet lined with parchment paper, lightly coated with EV olive oil. Bake for 15 minutes. Remove from oven and set aside.

For the Soup

¾ cup multigrain, low glycemic or gluten-free elbow macaroni pasta

2 tablespoons EV olive oil

1 cup diced onions

1 clove garlic, minced

6 cups low-sodium vegetable or chicken broth

¾ cup diced carrots

¾ cup diced celery

2 tablespoons chopped, fresh flat-leafed parsley

1 bay leaf

1 teaspoon fresh (or ¼ teaspoon dried) thyme

1 teaspoon sea salt

¼ teaspoon freshly ground black pepper

1 (14.5-ounce) can tomato sauce

2 cups chopped fresh spinach

- Cook the macaroni according to package directions (al dente). Drain, rinse well under cold water, drain again and set aside.

- In a large saucepan, sauté the onions in the olive oil until soft and caramelized (approximately 20 minutes). Add the garlic and cook for 1 more minute. Add the broth, vegetables, herbs and spices. Bring to a boil; reduce heat and simmer for 15 minutes. Add the tomato sauce and chopped spinach and simmer for 15 more minutes. Add the Dragon's eggs and cooked macaroni and simmer 10 minutes longer. Serve immediately.

This pasta dish is refreshing with its citrus highlights. Kids, try this Gremolata dressing on your favorite salad too.

Great Gremolata

Serves 4

Grated zest of 2 large
  lemons
Grated zest of 1 orange
1 clove garlic, minced
⅓ cup fresh flat-leafed
  parsley, chopped
1½ teaspoons lemon juice
¾ teaspoon sea salt
¼ teaspoon freshly
  ground black pepper
½ cup EV olive oil
1 pound multigrain, low
  glycemic or gluten-free
  linguine or angel hair
  pasta

- In a small saucepan, whisk together the lemon and orange zests, garlic, parsley, lemon juice, sea salt, pepper and olive oil. Heat mixture until just warm and turn off heat.

- In a large pot of boiling water salted water, cook the pasta according to package directions (al dente). Drain and toss with the infused olive oil (gremolata). Serve immediately.

Optional topping ingredients: tomato sauce, ground grass-fed bison, sliced red bell peppers and onions, and vegetable mozzarella cheese with a little bit of fresh garlic and Italian herbs.

Italian Flag Pizza (Margherita Pizza)

Serves 3-6

2 cups cooked couscous (for crust)

2 teaspoons dried parsley

¼ teaspoon granulated garlic

1 tablespoon EV olive oil

1 (7-ounce) package shredded vegetable
   mozzarella cheese

2 fresh tomatoes, thinly sliced

¼ cup chopped fresh basil

Dried oregano

Sea salt

Freshly ground black pepper

- To make 2 cups of cooked couscous, cook 1 cup dried couscous according to package directions, adding the dried parsley and granulated garlic to water. Add 1 tablespoon EV olive oil; stir and set aside to cool slightly.

- Preheat oven to 425°F. Very lightly grease a round pizza pan with some olive oil. Press the cooked couscous into the pan evenly, covering the base of the pan. Bake for 4 minutes. Remove pan from oven and cover couscous base with half of the cheese. Place the tomato slices and chopped fresh basil on top of cheese. Top with remaining cheese, and sprinkle with herbs and spices. Bake 15 minutes or until cheese is slightly browned in places. Using pizza cutter, cut into 6 pieces. Serve warm or cold.

Pasta! Sir Lexie's favorite

Add cooked, all-natural sliced chicken sausage for a meaty version. One of the great things about this delicious dish is that because there is virtually no fat (no dairy cheese), you don't have to wait to let it "set up" when it's finished cooking!

Lovable Lasagna

2 packages fresh or frozen chopped spinach

6 Roma tomatoes, halved, seeds removed

3 red bell peppers, cored, seeded and quartered

3 small zucchini squash, sliced

EV olive oil

Sea salt and freshly ground black pepper

Multigrain, low glycemic or gluten-free lasagna noodles

2-3 cups Quick & Tasty Tomato Sauce (page 38)

3 cups Tofu "Ricotta" Filling (page 43)

1½ cups shredded vegetable mozzarella cheese for topping

- If using frozen spinach, defrost, drain and squeeze out the juices. If using fresh spinach, steam for 1 minute, drain and squeeze out the juices. Set aside.

To Roast Vegetables
- Preheat oven to 350°F. Line one or two baking sheets with parchment paper and in a single layer, place tomato halves (skin side down), bell pepper quarters (skin side up), and zucchini slices on baking sheet. Drizzle with EV olive oil. Roast vegetables 45-50 minutes. Remove from oven and allow veggies to cool; remove skin from roasted peppers and slice the roasted vegetables into bite-sized pieces. Mix roasted vegetables and chopped spinach together; sprinkle with sea salt and black pepper. Set aside.

To Assemble Lasagna
- Cook lasagna noodles according to package directions (al dente). Rinse with cold water and drain. Lightly cover the bottom of a baking dish with some of the tomato sauce; top with a layer of lasagna noodles, slightly overlapping them. Top with a layer of roasted vegetables (half of them). Top with 1½ cups of tofu ricotta filling followed by a layer of noodles. Spread some of the tomato sauce over that layer, followed by the last half of the roasted vegetables. Top with the remaining 1½ cups of tofu ricotta filling, and the remaining noodles. Spread remaining tomato sauce over the noodles and top with shredded vegetable mozzarella cheese.

- Cover and bake in 350°F oven for 40 minutes. Uncover and bake another 10 minutes. Remove from oven; serve immediately.

"Our hairdresser, Lisa Pratti, has a favorite manicotti recipe that her Italian grandmother, Lucy, used to make for her. Here it is, dressed up, healthy and delicious!"

— Lexie & Alice

Lucy's Manicotti

Serves 4-6

1 (8-ounce) box multi-grain, gluten-free or low glycemic manicotti shells (14 pieces)
1 pound ground grass-fed bison
2 tablespoons EV olive oil
1 (9-ounce) package fresh spinach, cooked, cooled, drained and chopped
2 egg whites
1 package shredded vegetable mozzarella cheese (divided)
2 cloves garlic, minced
2 tablespoons chopped fresh (or 1 teaspoon dried) basil
1 tablespoon chopped fresh (or ½ teaspoon dried) oregano
¾ teaspoon sea salt
½ teaspoon freshly ground black pepper
3-4 cups Quick & Tasty Tomato Sauce (page 38)

- Cook manicotti pasta according to package directions (al dente). Rinse and set aside. In a medium bowl, combine the uncooked ground bison, EV olive oil, cooked spinach, egg whites, ½ of the vegetable mozzarella, and the herbs and spices. Toss gently with a fork until well combined.

- Preheat oven to 350°F. In a (9 x13) baking pan, spread 1 cup of tomato sauce. Stuff each manicotti with the filling and place in baking pan on top of sauce. Top with remaining 2-3 cups tomato sauce. Cover with aluminum foil and cook for 40 minutes.

- Remove foil, sprinkle top of manicotti with remaining vegetable mozzarella and continue to cook, uncovered, for 10-12 minutes. Serve hot.

Mac & Cheese with Broccoli

Serves 4

1½ cups chopped broccoli

1½ cups multigrain, low glycemic or gluten-free pasta of choice

1 tablespoon EV olive oil

¼ cup trans fat free buttery spread or ghee

1½ tablespoons whole spelt flour

1½ cups soy or rice milk

1½ cups shredded vegetable mozzarella cheese

4 slices vegetable pepper jack or Swiss cheese, broken into pieces

⅛ teaspoon paprika

½ teaspoon ground mustard

½ teaspoon sea salt

⅛ teaspoon freshly ground black pepper

- Steam chopped broccoli for 2 minutes or until 'crisp tender'. Drain and place broccoli in ice water, drain again. Set aside.

- Cook pasta according to package directions (al dente). Drain. While pasta is cooking, place EV olive oil and buttery spread or ghee in a large saucepan. Add the flour and on medium high heat, stir until slightly thickened like a smooth paste. Whisk in the soy or rice milk and cook, stirring, until the mixture begins to thicken, 3-4 minutes. Add the broccoli, veggie cheeses and seasonings and stir until the cheese is melted and the sauce is smooth. Add more warmed soy milk if necessary. Stir in the pasta and serve warm.

Pretty Pasta (with Asparagus, Chicken & Tomatoes)

Serves 4

2 boneless, skinless chicken breasts

EV olive oil

Lemon pepper, sea salt and granulated garlic (for seasoning chicken)

1 bunch asparagus spears (tough bottom ends removed), chopped (3-inch)

2 cloves garlic, peeled & sliced

Sea salt and freshly ground black pepper

2 teaspoons fresh lemon juice

½ pound multigrain, low glycemic or gluten-free pasta (fettuccini, penne, or vermicelli)

1 (14.5-ounce) can diced tomatoes, with juices

2 tablespoons chopped fresh basil

½ cup shredded vegetable mozzarella cheese

- Preheat oven to 400°F. Rinse chicken breasts and pat dry. Place them individually between two layers of plastic wrap or into a zip-lock bag not completely sealed to let air escape. Flatten chicken breasts slightly with a mallet (or whatever works, such as a can of tomatoes). Remove from bag, drizzle lightly with EV olive oil and season both sides with lemon pepper, sea salt, and granulated garlic. Place on parchment or foil-lined baking pan. Bake for 11-13 minutes until no longer pink inside. Remove from oven; cover and set aside.

- Cook pasta according to package directions (al dente). Drain pasta but keep a little bit of the water in the pasta to keep it from sticking together.

- Heat a large skillet until very warm; add 2 tablespoons EV olive oil followed immediately by chopped asparagus, garlic slices, sea salt and black pepper. Stir-fry 7 minutes, remove from heat and add the lemon juice.

- Pull the baked chicken breasts apart into bite-sized pieces. Return the skillet with the asparagus to the burner and heat to medium high; add the diced tomatoes and their juices and the fresh basil and simmer on medium low for 3 minutes. Add the chicken, drained pasta and cheese. Toss and serve immediately.

Sesame Soy Nut Pasta

Serves 2-4

2 green onions, thinly sliced (divided)

2 teaspoons minced fresh ginger

1 small clove garlic, minced

½ cup salt-free vegetable broth

3 tablespoons soy nut butter

1 tablespoon plus 1 teaspoon liquid aminos seasoning

1 teaspoon sesame oil

⅛ teaspoon cayenne pepper (optional)

⅛ teaspoon sea salt

8 ounces multigrain, low glycemic or gluten-free pasta (linguini, spaghetti, or angel hair)

- In a heavy saucepan, combine the first 9 ingredients (including only half of the green onions). Cook on medium heat until smooth and blended, stirring occasionally. Set aside.

- In a large pot of boiling salted water, cook pasta according to the package directions (al dente). Drain well.

- If necessary reheat the sesame-soy nut butter mixture. Pour over the cooked pasta, sprinkle with remaining green onion slices and serve immediately.

pasta! Sir Lexie's favorite

Kids will love helping to make this quick and tasty pasta salad.

Twirly Tuna Pasta

Serves 4

1½ cups (12 ounces) dried multigrain, low-glycemic or gluten-free fusilli or rotini pasta

Handful of fresh green beans, cut in half, or ¾ cup frozen peas

3 (3-ounce) cans chunk light or solid white tuna packed in water, drained

¼ cup EV olive oil

1 tablespoon chia seeds

2 teaspoons chopped fresh, flat-leafed parsley

2 teaspoons grated lemon zest

2½ tablespoons fresh lemon juice

1 clove garlic, minced

Sea salt and freshly ground black pepper

- Cook pasta according to package directions (al dente), adding peas or green beans in the last 2 minutes of cooking.

- Meanwhile, in a large serving bowl, combine tuna, olive oil, chia seeds, parsley, lemon zest, lemon juice, and garlic. Season with sea salt and black pepper to taste. Drain pasta and beans or peas and fold into the tuna mixture. Stir to combine; adjust seasonings and/or olive oil and lemon juice to taste. Serve warm, at room temperature, or chilled.

For Our Siblings

Because they deserve the best!
(And kids with cancer may safely eat these recipes too!)

In the day-to-day life of a cancer family, the focus is typically on the person who is sick. We seldom think about anybody else who could be affected, like the brothers or sisters in the family. We might think that their lives wouldn't be changed by the illness but they really are; almost as much as the cancer patient's life is affected, just in a different way. They often feel forgotten and left behind. Such as a day when the whole family is planning to go to their soccer game or dance recital and then all of a sudden, in a blink of an eye, the sibling has to be brought to their special event by a friend because the family is busy spending time in the hospital with the patient. They don't just feel left behind and forgotten; but they also feel jealous - such as when the child with cancer gets all sorts of prizes and gifts and the sibling gets a pencil if he or she is lucky.

In our family we try to include my sister, Emily, as much as possible even though sometimes we can't always be there for her. Once we had to miss her dance recital because I was in the hospital with the chicken pox; though we did try to make it up to her as much as possible.

So we've included a chapter for our brothers and sisters. These are some recipes that some of them have really enjoyed. This chapter is for all of our siblings who sacrifice so much for us!

- Lexie

To get nice stiff peaks in your egg whites, be sure that no yolk sneaks into the bowl as you separate the egg. This light, fluffy and delicious cake tastes even better the second day!

Blueberry Picnic Cake

Serves 8

6 egg whites
¾ cup coconut crystals (divided)
½ cup softened ghee
2 tablespoons canola oil
¼ teaspoon sea salt
1 teaspoon pure vanilla extract
1 cup white spelt flour
½ cup whole spelt flour
1 teaspoon baking powder
  (cornstarch-free)
⅓ cup soy or rice milk
1½ cups fresh or frozen
   blueberries coated in
   2 teaspoons flour
Ceylon cinnamon for topping

- Preheat oven to 350°F. In a deep glass or metal bowl, beat egg whites until stiff peaks form. Beat in ¼ cup of the coconut crystals. Set aside.

- In a separate mixing bowl, using an electric mixer, combine the ghee, canola oil, salt, vanilla extract and remaining ½ cup coconut crystals. In a separate bowl, combine the flours and baking powder and add the dry mixture to the ghee mixture alternately with the soy or rice milk, stirring with a wooden spoon until well blended. Fold in the stiffly beaten egg whites until well blended. Fold in the blueberries coated in flour.

- Pour mixture into a parchment-lined square (8 x 8) baking pan. Sprinkle with Ceylon cinnamon and bake for 35-40 minutes or until a toothpick inserted in center comes out clean. Transfer cake pan to wire rack to cool. Wrap leftovers and store in refrigerator. This cake may be frozen.

Chicken Toes with Sweet Mustard Dipping Sauce

Serves 2-4

2½ cups dried breadcrumbs (yeast-free)
EV olive oil
Sea salt and freshly ground black pepper
2-3 skinless, boneless chicken breasts
½ cup egg wash (3 egg whites with
   3 tablespoons water, whisk well)

2 teaspoons fresh (or ½ teaspoon dried)
  thyme
½ teaspoon sea salt
¼ teaspoon freshly ground black pepper
1 tablespoon chia seeds
⅛ teaspoon cayenne pepper (optional)

- Preheat oven to 375°F. To make dried bread crumbs, place fresh Irish Soda Bread cubes (page 35), or other yeast-free bread cubes onto parchment or foil-lined baking pan; drizzle with EV olive oil and sprinkle with sea salt and freshly ground black pepper. Bake for 15 minutes, flipping once halfway through. Croutons should be golden and crunchy. Crush into crumbs in food processor once cooled.

- Rinse chicken breasts and pat dry. Slice each chicken breast in half and cut evenly into short strips. Dip strips into shallow bowl of the egg wash.

- In a separate shallow bowl, combine the bread crumbs, thyme, salt, black pepper, chia seeds and cayenne pepper. Place chicken toes that have been coated in egg wash into the bread crumb mixture a few at a time, and turn to coat evenly.

- Preheat oven to 400°F. Place chicken strips on parchment-lined baking sheet. Bake for 11 minutes. While chicken is baking, prepare the dipping sauce.

Sweet Mustard Dipping Sauce
⅓ cup coconut nectar
¼ cup mustard (vinegar-free such as Coleman's®)
2 teaspoons lime juice

- Whisk the coconut nectar, mustard and lime juice together in a small bowl and stir until well blended. Serve chicken toes warm with dipping sauce.

For Our Siblings

Oven simmering provides even cooking of this thick chili, as opposed to the fluctuating temperature that some stovetops produce. A crock pot is always an option following initial sautéing.

Chili X 2

Serves 6-8

Veggie Version
2 tablespoons EV olive oil
I large red or sweet Vidalia onion, diced
2-3 cloves garlic, minced
3 jalapeño peppers, stemmed, seeded, and finely chopped
I green bell pepper, stemmed, seeded and diced
I red bell pepper, stemmed, seeded and diced
2 large celery ribs, diced
2 teaspoons chopped fresh (or ½ teaspoon dried) oregano
⅛ teaspoon Ceylon cinnamon
3 tablespoons chili powder
I tablespoon ground cumin

I teaspoon sea salt
½ teaspoon freshly ground black pepper
Sprinkle of red pepper flakes (optional)
I large bay leaf
I (28-ounce) can diced tomatoes, un-drained
2 tablespoons tomato paste
2 cups vegetable broth
I (15.5-ounce) can black or kidney beans, drained
Add I cup cooked edamame
Juice of one lime
2 tablespoons fresh cilantro
I small zucchini, diced
2 tablespoons ghee
2 chopped green onions, avocado slices and lime wedges for topping

- Preheat oven to 300°F. Heat a large oven-proof heavy skillet or stockpot on the stove top. Add the olive oil and diced onions and sauté on medium low for 15 minutes. Add the minced garlic and sauté for 2 more minutes. Add the peppers and celery; blend well and sauté another 5 minutes. In a small bowl blend the herbs, spices and pepper flakes together and add to the vegetable mixture along with the bay leaf. Stir to blend. Add the tomatoes and tomato paste, vegetable broth and beans; stir, cover and cook in preheated oven for 1 hour, adding more broth if needed. Add the lime juice, cilantro and zucchini and return pot to oven and cook for 1 more hour. Remove bay leaf, add ghee and stir until melted. Serve topped with green onions, avocado slices and lime wedges.

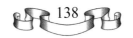

Meaty Version

- After heating the skillet and adding the EV olive oil, and prior to sautéing the diced onion, sear on high heat 1 pound boneless chicken thighs trimmed of fat and diced into bite-sized pieces. Transfer meat to a bowl. To the skillet, add 1 pound ground bison and brown on high heat for 2 minutes, turning as needed; transfer to same bowl as chicken thighs. Cook remaining recipe as above, adding browned chicken and bison along with tomatoes.

This recipe is fun for kids to make themselves - to treat their siblings to a special breakfast in bed!

Perfect Parfait

Serves 2

½ cup rolled oats, old-fashioned, uncooked
¼ teaspoon Ceylon cinnamon
½ cup raw sunflower or pumpkin seeds
1 tablespoon coconut crystals

½ cup fresh blueberries
6 fresh strawberries, sliced
1 unripe banana, sliced
1 kiwi fruit, peeled and sliced
1 cup dairy-free frozen vanilla dessert of choice

- To toast the granola, preheat oven to 350°F. Place rolled oats, cinnamon and sunflower or pumpkin seeds on a parchment or foil-lined baking pan. Cook for 7 minutes or until golden. Remove from oven and mix with coconut crystals. Set aside.

- In each of two parfait dish or drinking glasses, layer ingredients as desired. Serve immediately.

Spicy Rice Pilaf

Serves 4-6

2 tablespoons EV olive oil

1 tablespoon ghee

½ cup multigrain, low glycemic or gluten-free vermicelli or spaghetti pasta,
   broken into ½-inch pieces

1 cup long-grain brown rice

2½ cups low-sodium chicken broth, heated

2 tablespoons fresh (or 2 teaspoons dried) flat-leafed parsley

¼ teaspoon red pepper flakes (optional)

½ teaspoon sea salt

¼ teaspoon freshly ground black pepper

1 cup frozen peas

- Place the olive oil and ghee in a large skillet and heat until ghee is melted. Add the pasta pieces and sauté until nicely browned, stirring constantly to prevent burning. Add the rice and continue sautéing, stirring constantly until rice is slightly browned (3 minutes). Add the heated broth (carefully to avoid steam burns), parsley, and spices. Stir, and then cover immediately. Cook on low for 50 minutes without lifting cover.

- When the chicken broth is absorbed and the rice is soft, add the peas; remove from heat and let rest, covered, for 10 minutes. Fluff with a fork before serving.

Smoothies!

We dedicated a chapter exclusively to smoothies because they are fun, delicious, healthy, and very soothing. You can use your imagination with all sorts of fruits and vegetables, rice or soy milk, green tea, and for some rich "ice cream-like" flavor, try a small scoop of your favorite low glycemic, dairy-free frozen vanilla dessert in your fruit smoothies.

Soothing and invigorating at the same time!

Be My Valentine Smoothie

Serves 3-4

2 teaspoons very finely chopped fresh mint
½ teaspoon peppermint extract
2 cup chilled green or white tea
2 cups chilled rice or soy milk
I cup drained silken tofu
I cup dairy-free frozen dessert of choice (vanilla or mint)
10 ice cubes

• Combine all ingredients in a blender, cover and pulse until well-blended. Pour into tall drinking glasses and top with a sprig of fresh mint; serve immediately.

Smoothies!

Cherries are rich in antioxidants, Vitamins A and C, and fiber. They also contain melatonin and potassium and other minerals. They help to fight infections and are a high alkaline (friendly) food.

Bing Cherry Smoothie

Serves 2

1½ cups chopped, pitted frozen fresh Bing cherries

1 cup unsweetened cherry juice, frozen or freshly squeezed

½ cup chilled rice or soy milk

¼ cup almond milk

1 cup drained silken tofu

½ teaspoon almond extract

2 tablespoons coconut nectar

6 ice cubes

- Place all ingredients in a blender and pulse until smooth. Pour into two tall glasses and serve immediately.

Smoothies!

Blackberry Dream Cloud Smoothie

Serves 3-4

2 cups fresh blackberries

1 cup frozen strawberries, roughly chopped

1 cup pomegranate juice from concentrate

1 cup drained silken tofu

6 ice cubes

1 cup dairy-free frozen vanilla dessert of choice (divided)

- Place all ingredients except for the frozen vanilla dessert in a large blender and pulse until well blended. Add ½ cup of the frozen vanilla dessert. Pulse until blended. Pour into large serving glasses and top with a dollop of remaining frozen vanilla dessert. Serve immediately.

Smoothies!

Blueberry Moon Delight Smoothie

Serves 2-3

½ cup chilled cranberry juice, unsweetened

½ cup chilled blueberry juice, unsweetened

¾ cup chilled plum juice, unsweetened

2 cups frozen blueberries

1 cup chilled soy or rice milk

1 cup drained silken tofu

- Mix the juices and frozen blueberries in a blender, pulsing until smooth. Add the soy or rice milk and the tofu; blend until smooth. Pour into tall drinking glasses and serve with a straw.

Powerful antioxidants, great flavor and very soothing!

Green Tea Smoothie

Serves 2-3

2 green or white tea bags of choice
1 cup very hot water
¾ cup fresh or frozen raspberries
¾ cup fresh or frozen blueberries

1 unripe banana
2 tablespoons coconut nectar
6 ice cubes

- Steep the tea in the hot water and cool to room temperature. Place cooled tea and remaining ingredients including the ice cubes in a blender and pulse until smooth. Pour into tall glasses and serve immediately.

Smoothies!

Kyle Picard says, "I created this smoothie to have as a snack and increase my daily calorie intake since I am underweight for my age. Since my brain tumor I have been eating as healthy as I can while trying to gain weight. I hope you will treat yourself to my delicious [organic] smoothie and enjoy it as much as I do."

Kyle's Smoothie

Serves 3

1 handful tender chopped Swiss chard or collard
    greens with stem removed
6 strawberries (fresh or frozen)
¼ cup blueberries (fresh or frozen)
3 ounces Oki (such as Orenda International®),
    a concentrated berry drink with aronia berry
    (rich in antioxidants and flavenoids)
1 cup vanilla coconut milk ice cream
    1 serving (17 grams) brown rice protein powder
    with water (see directions on container)

- Put all ingredients in a high speed blender or a food processor and purée until fully mixed and smooth. Top with ground flaxseed if you'd like and serve immediately.

Sunrise Smoothie

Serves 2-4

2 cups chilled soy or rice milk
2 cups fresh strawberries
1 cup frozen blueberries
1 avocado, cubed

½ cup freshly squeezed orange juice
1 tablespoon coconut nectar
5 ice cubes

• Place all ingredients in a blender and pulse until well blended. Serve immediately.

This is an old-fashioned comfort food and though new to some kids, will soon become a favorite !

Comforting Cabbage Rolls

Makes 14-16 Rolls

1 large head of green cabbage

Sauce
1 tablespoon ghee
1 medium yellow onion, chopped
1 clove garlic, minced
1 (28-ounce) can diced tomatoes with juices
½ cup soy or rice milk

1 tablespoon lemon juice
1 tablespoon coconut crystals or
    coconut nectar
Sea salt and freshly ground black pepper
    to taste

- Melt ghee in a heavy saucepan over medium heat. Add the chopped onion and sauté for 7 minutes, covered, stirring occasionally. Reduce heat to medium low; add the garlic and cook, stirring, for 2 minutes. Add the tomatoes/juices and simmer for 5 minutes. Add the soy or rice milk and simmer on medium heat, stirring occasionally for 5 more minutes. Add the lemon juice and coconut crystals; simmer 5 minutes. Remove from heat and adjust seasoning to taste. Set aside.

Comforting Cabbage Rolls, continued

Filling

¾ cup cooked brown rice, cooled

1 tablespoon ghee

1 cup finely chopped yellow onion

2 medium cloves garlic, minced

¾ pound uncooked ground grass-fed bison

¾ pound uncooked ground turkey

2 tablespoons fresh, flat-leafed parsley, chopped

1 teaspoon paprika

½ teaspoon dried oregano

½ teaspoon cinnamon

3 slices vegetable pepper jack or Swiss cheese, broken into little pieces

1 large egg white

½ teaspoon sea salt

¼ teaspoon freshly ground black pepper

- Cook rice as directed and set aside to cool. In a skillet, melt the ghee over medium-high heat. Add the onions and simmer, covered, about 5 minutes. Reduce heat to medium low, add the garlic and cook for 1 minute, remove from heat and cool slightly. In a large bowl, combine the remaining filling ingredients and add the cooked onions and garlic and mix well.

To Prepare Cabbage Leaves
- Set aside a large plate for the cabbage leaves. Carefully core the cabbage by using a sharp paring knife and carefully making a cut around the perimeter of the stem about 1½-inch deep. This will allow the leaves to be peeled away easily after they are steamed. (The stem of the cabbage is very hard so care must be taken to avoid cutting yourself.) Place the cabbage, core end down, in a large kettle filled with about two inches of water. Cover kettle and bring to a boil, reduce heat to medium and steam cabbage for about 5 minutes. Remove the cabbage from the kettle with large tongs and peel away a few of the leaves gently without tearing them and layer them onto the plate. With the tongs, return the remaining cabbage head to the steaming pot, core end down, and steam another 5 minutes, remove cabbage from kettle with tongs again and remove a few more leaves. Repeat this process until you have removed approximately 14-16 leaves. The leaves should be cooked al dente and pliable enough to roll.

To Fill and Cook
- Preheat oven to 300°F. Spoon ½ cup of the sauce into the bottom of an oven-proof casserole dish (covered) or line the bottom of the dish with leftover cabbage leaves. Depending on the size of the leaf, spoon 2 tablespoons to ½ cup of filling into the center of each cabbage leaf. Fold bottom of leaf over filling, fold in each side tightly and roll to top of leaf to form a neat cylinder.

- Form all cabbage rolls and pack them tightly in the casserole dish. Cover with two-thirds of the sauce and bake until the meat is cooked through and the rolls are tender, approximately 2 hours. Serve immediately with remaining (warmed) sauce.

Cauli-Jolly Christmas Tree Appetizer

Serves 6-8

1 bunch broccoli flowerets
1 cucumber slice for star and 1 for trunk
1 bunch cauliflower flowerets
4-6 cherry tomatoes
½ red bell pepper, sliced
4 radishes

- Assemble the broccoli flowerets in the shape of a Christmas tree. Cut a piece of cucumber for trunk of tree; place the cauliflower flowerets at base for snow effect, cherry tomatoes on tree as ornaments and red bell pepper slices as garland. Quarter radishes (for gifts under tree). Using a star cookie cutter, shape the cucumber and place it on the top of the tree. Serve with Pimento and Green Pepper Dip (below).

Pimento and Green Pepper Dip
1 cup silken tofu
1 tablespoon coconut nectar
1 tablespoon rice or soy milk
1 teaspoon sea salt
1 teaspoon lemon juice
¼ teaspoon freshly ground black pepper
1 small clove garlic, minced
3 tablespoons chopped pimentos, well drained
3 tablespoons finely chopped green bell peppers

- Squeeze liquid out of tofu with clean white dishcloth. Place all ingredients in small food processor and pulse until creamy. Chill for at least 2 hours before serving.

"I love pistachio muffins, but pistachios are not a healthy nut due to their high mold susceptibility and they are an acidic food. So, we've substituted with delicious pine nuts and macadamia nuts."

— Lexie

Make Believe Muffins

Makes 8-10 medium muffins

¾ cup whole wheat flour
I cup white spelt flour
½ cup coconut crystals
½ cup old-fashioned oats
½ teaspoon Ceylon cinnamon
½ cup chopped pine nuts
½ cup chopped raw macadamia nuts
I tablespoon baking powder (cornstarch-free)
½ teaspoon sea salt
I cup rice or soy milk
⅓ cup canola oil
2 tablespoons melted ghee
¼ cup barley malt syrup
4 egg whites
I teaspoon pure vanilla extract
Extra pine nuts for topping

- Preheat oven to 400°F. Mix flours, coconut crystals, oats, cinnamon, pine nuts, macadamia nuts, baking powder and sea salt in bowl, stirring with spoon until well blended. Add rice or soy milk, oil, melted ghee, barley malt syrup, egg whites and vanilla extract. Stir lightly just to mix.

- Spoon batter into paper-lined muffin cups. Sprinkle pine nuts over top of batter. Bake for 20 minutes or until toothpick inserted in center comes out clean. Cool 5 minutes; remove from pan and cool on wire rack.

Warms you from head to toe.

Mexican Hot Chocolate

Serves 4

¼ cup unsweetened cocoa powder, sifted
¼ cup coconut crystals
4½ cups rice or soy milk
¾ teaspoon ground Ceylon cinnamon
Slight sprinkling of cayenne pepper (optional)
1 cup dairy-free frozen vanilla dessert of choice (divided)
½ teaspoon pure vanilla extract

- Mix the cocoa powder, coconut crystals, rice or soy milk, cinnamon and cayenne in a medium sauce-pan. Cook over medium heat, whisking constantly, until the coconut crystals are dissolved and the ingredients are well-blended and warm. Add ½ cup frozen vanilla dessert and continue to heat and blend with the whisk until simmering. Remove from the heat and add the vanilla extract.

- Serve piping hot in 4 mugs and top with remaining frozen vanilla dessert.

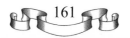

This recipe is made with steel-cut oats because we like their hearty, chewy texture, but they take a long time to cook unless you partially cook the night before as is described on the label. The glycemic index and nutritional goodness are not much different than old-fashioned oats (42 versus 50) that take less than half the time to cook, so this recipe may be made with old-fashioned oats, following the label's cooking time and instructions. There are about 5 grams of protein in a serving of this low-fat porridge but it is loaded with much-needed and healthy (low-processed) carbohydrates.

New Year's Day Porridge

Serves 4

2 cups water
2 cups soy or rice milk
¼ teaspoon sea salt (or to taste)
I cup steel-cut oats
I teaspoon ghee
¼ cup blueberries or chopped plums or pears
2 tablespoons coconut nectar

- Combine the water, soy or rice milk and sea salt in a large, heavy saucepan; bring to a boil. Slowly add the oats, stirring constantly. Reduce the heat to low, cover and simmer 20 minutes, stirring occasionally with a wooden spoon. Stir in the ghee. Cover, and continue to simmer for another 15-20 minutes, stirring often to prevent the cereal from sticking to the bottom of the pan, until the oats are soft and the mixture is creamy. Remove from heat and add coconut nectar. Serve with added fruit (if desired) and drizzle with a little more coconut nectar. Serve immediately. Refrigerate and reheat as desired.

- Porridge can also be frozen. Line ice cube trays with plastic wrap and fill each cube with oatmeal; cover with plastic wrap and freeze. Once frozen solid, remove the cubes from the ice tray and freeze in a plastic bag. For each portion, thaw 3 or 4 cubes and re-heat by placing them in an oven-proof dish in a pre-heated 300°F oven for 10 minutes, adding a little bit of water. Add warm soy milk and fruit if desired.

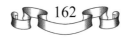

Similar to American Chop Suey - this is a kid pleaser!

Snow Day Pasta

Serves 6-8

1¾ cups multigrain, low glycemic or gluten-free pasta
3 tablespoons EV olive oil
1 medium onion, chopped
1 green bell pepper, diced
1 red bell pepper, diced
1 pound ground grass-fed bison
1 teaspoon sea salt
½ teaspoon freshly ground black pepper
1 tablespoon fresh (or 1 teaspoon dried) oregano
3 medium cloves garlic, minced
1 (28-ounce) can diced tomatoes
2 tablespoons ghee (optional)
Chopped scallions for topping

- Cook pasta according to package directions (al dente). In a large skillet, sauté the onions and peppers in the EV olive oil until soft. Add the ground bison, herbs, spices and garlic and cook until browned. Add the diced tomatoes and simmer while the pasta is cooking. Drain the pasta and add it to the skillet with the ghee and stir to blend. Top with chopped scallions and serve piping hot.

Cooking this bison stew in the oven provides even, slow cooking and guarantees tender meat and vegetables. It is hearty, yummy, and full of protein, antioxidants and warm goodness.

Superman Stew (Bison Stew)

Serves 6-8

2½ pounds grass-fed bison steak,
   cut into 1½-inch cubes
Sea salt and freshly ground black pepper
3 tablespoons EV olive oil
1 large yellow onion (about 2 cups),
   coarsely chopped
3 cloves garlic, minced
3 tablespoons spelt flour
3 cups low-sodium chicken broth

2 bay leaves
1 tablespoon finely chopped fresh
   (or ⅓ teaspoon dried) thyme
¼ teaspoon Ceylon cinnamon
3-4 medium red potatoes cut into 1-inch cubes
4 large carrots, sliced ½-inch thick
1 cup frozen or fresh peas
½ cup finely chopped fresh
   (or 2 tablespoons dried) flat-leafed parsley

- Preheat oven to 300°F. Season cubed bison steak with sea salt and black pepper. Heat 1 tablespoon EV olive oil in large ovenproof kettle over medium-high heat. Add half of the meat to the pot; brown for 1 minute. Turn meat and brown other side for 1 minute. Transfer partially cooked meat to bowl. Add 1 tablespoon EV olive oil to pan and repeat browning process with remaining cubed bison steak. Place in bowl with first batch and set aside.

- Reduce heat to medium. Add remaining tablespoon of oil to kettle; add the chopped onion. Cook, stirring frequently and scraping the bottom of the pan with a wooden spoon to loosen browned bits until the onions have softened, approximately 5 minutes. Add the garlic and continue to cook for 1 minute. Stir in the flour and cook for approximately 3 minutes. Add the chicken broth slowly, stirring until mixture thickens. Add the bay leaves, thyme, and Ceylon cinnamon; bring to a simmer. Return the meat and its juices to the pot; cover kettle and place in oven and cook for 45 minutes.

- Remove kettle from oven and add the potatoes and carrots. Cover and return the kettle to the oven; cook just until the vegetables are tender, about 1 hour. Remove kettle from oven and add peas and parsley and let stand for 5 minutes. Discard the bay leaves and adjust seasonings to taste. Serve immediately.

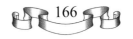

With carrots, celery, potatoes, green beans, red bell pepper and other immune- boosting ingredients like onions, garlic and parsley, this comfort food packs a healthy punch! Since making chicken pot pie usually takes a long time (roasting a chicken, preparing stock, vegetables and crust), we've simplified it and made it healthier by using boneless, skinless chicken breasts, or you could use a pre-cooked rotisserie chicken from your local grocery store. To save time even further, cook the chicken and/or make the gravy the night before serving. Parents, you will find that the gravy is thin and plentiful when you pour the mixture over the vegetables. This will thicken while cooking.

Starry Sky Chicken Pot Pie

Serves 6

For Chicken
2 boneless, skinless chicken breasts
EV olive oil

½ teaspoon each dried sage,
    thyme and rosemary
Sea salt and freshly ground black pepper

Starry Sky Chicken Pot Pie, continued

- Preheat oven to 400°F. Rinse chicken breasts and pat dry. Place them individually between two layers of plastic wrap or wax paper or in a zip-lock bag not completely sealed to let air escape. Flatten the chicken breasts slightly with a mallet (or whatever works). Remove from bag and drizzle with olive oil; sprinkle both sides with seasonings and place on a parchment or foil-lined baking pan. Bake for 11-13 minutes. Remove from oven, cover and set aside to cool. Shred chicken by hand when cooled.

For Vegetables

⅓ cup diced red bell pepper

½ cup diced carrots

⅓ cup diced potatoes

⅓ cup diced celery

½ cup diced onions

½ cup chopped green beans

2 cloves garlic, minced

2 tablespoons chopped fresh
   (or 2 teaspoons dried) flat-leafed parsley

2 teaspoons fresh (or ½ teaspoon dried)
   thyme

- Fill bottom half of steam pot with water. Place carrots in top half of covered steam pot. Bring to a boil; reduce heat and steam on medium high for 5 minutes. Add the red bell peppers, potatoes, celery and onions and continue steaming for 8 minutes. Add the green beans and steam another 5 minutes. Remove from heat and add remaining ingredients. Set aside.

For Roux/Gravy

2 tablespoons EV olive oil

4 tablespoons ghee

¼ cup plus 1 tablespoon whole wheat flour

4½ cups low-sodium chicken broth

2 teaspoons poultry seasoning

½ teaspoon sea salt

¼ teaspoon freshly ground black pepper

- Heat the olive oil and ghee in a large saucepan until ghee is melted. Add the flour and whisk occasionally for 3 minutes. Slowly whisk in the broth, add the seasonings and stir occasionally as it thickens. Simmer for 15 minutes. Add the vegetables and chicken to this mixture and set aside.

For Starry Sky Topping

½ batch Billowy Biscuits dough (page 29), cut into star shapes on well floured surface.

To Assemble & Cook Pie

- Preheat oven to 450°F. Place vegetable mixture into a square (9 x 9) baking pan or round casserole dish. Pour gravy over vegetables and bake, uncovered, for 15 minutes. Remove from oven (if dish is shallow, be careful not to slosh the hot liquid onto yourself) and top with biscuit dough stars; quickly brush stars with egg wash (egg white whisked well with 2 tablespoons water). Bake another 15 minutes or until biscuit stars are cooked through and pie is slightly bubbling. Carefully remove pie from oven (very hot!). Let pie sit for 15 minutes before serving.

Broccoli Fish Bundles

Serves 6

18 broccoli spears
6 slices vegetable pepper jack or Swiss cheese
6 haddock, cod or salmon fillets
⅛ teaspoon lemon pepper seasoning
⅓ cup ghee, melted
I tablespoon fresh lemon juice
I garlic clove, minced
¼ teaspoon sea salt
⅛ teaspoon freshly ground black pepper

- Steam broccoli for 3 minutes or until crisp tender. Drain and place broccoli in ice water, drain again.

- Preheat oven to 350°F. To make bundles, place 1 slice of cheese over 3 broccoli spears and wrap with a fish fillet and fasten with a toothpick. Place bundles on a parchment or foil-lined baking pan. Sprinkle with lemon pepper and bake for 15-20 minutes or until fish flakes easily with a fork. Meanwhile, combine the melted ghee, lemon juice, garlic, salt and black pepper.

- Transfer fish bundles to a serving platter, remove toothpicks and drizzle with warmed ghee mixture. Serve immediately.

Remember to cook the rice early in the day (or the day before) to ensure that it is well chilled when preparing the fried rice.

Chicken Fried Rice

Serves 4-6

3 cups cooked brown rice, chilled
3 egg whites with 2 tablespoons water
EV olive oil or canola oil
3 green onions, finely chopped
1½ cups (in total) chopped fresh vegetables
   (mixture such as broccoli, sugar snap peas,
   green beans, red bell pepper)
1 teaspoon minced fresh ginger (peeled)
1 pound ground chicken

½ teaspoon sea salt
½ teaspoon freshly ground black pepper
2 cloves garlic, minced
3 tablespoons liquid aminos seasoning
1 teaspoon sesame oil
1 teaspoon coconut nectar
Chopped green onions or fresh flat-leafed
   parsley for topping

- With your hands, break up and loosen the cold cooked rice (wet your hands first). Lightly beat the egg whites with 2 tablespoons water. Set aside.

- Preheat a large, deep skillet or wok on medium high. Add 1 tablespoon EV olive oil or canola oil; add the chopped green onions with the mixture of vegetables and the minced ginger and stir fry for 3 minutes, stirring and lifting continuously. Transfer vegetables to a bowl.

- Turn heat to high; add 2 tablespoons EV olive oil and the ground chicken, sea salt, black pepper and minced garlic. Stir fry for 3 minutes. Drain and transfer meat to a separate bowl.

- With pan still on high, add 2 tablespoons EV olive oil or canola oil and the rice. Heat rice thoroughly, turning it in a folding motion with a spatula so that it heats evenly and doesn't stick to the pan.

- Return the vegetables and ground chicken to the pan with the rice, folding all ingredients together until blended. Add the liquid aminos seasoning, sesame oil and coconut nectar. Fold in the egg whites and water mixture with a spatula and turn off heat just as the eggs begin to set. Serve hot and garnished with chopped green onions or chopped flat-leafed parsley.

In this recipe, any orange will do, but if you can find Cara Cara oranges, give them a try - they're delicious!

Meal-in-One Salad

Serves 4-6

2 boneless, skinless chicken breasts
Sea salt and freshly ground black pepper &
  seasonings of choice
½ cup raw macadamia nuts, toasted,
  coarsely chopped
1 head Romaine lettuce
1 small bunch fresh spinach

1 cup fresh broccoli, chopped
½ cup red bell pepper, sliced
½ European cucumber, sliced
2 green onions, chopped
1 Cara Cara orange, peeled, segments
  quartered

To Cook Chicken

• Preheat oven to 400°F. Rinse chicken breasts and pat dry. Place them individually between two layers of plastic wrap or in a zip-lock bag not completely sealed to let air escape. Flatten the chicken breasts slightly with a mallet or whatever works such as a can of tomatoes. Remove from bag; drizzle with olive oil and season with sea salt, black pepper and your favorite seasonings (Italian blend or Herbs de Provence work well) and place on a parchment or foil-lined baking pan. Bake for 11-13 minutes. Remove from oven, cover and set aside.

To Roast Macadamia Nuts

• Reduce oven temperature to 350°F. Place macadamia nuts on a parchment or foil-lined baking pan. Toast in oven for 4 minutes. Remove from oven and set aside to cool.

To Prepare Salad

• Break up the lettuce and spinach into bite-sized pieces and place in a large serving dish. Top with remaining ingredients, ending with chicken pieces and chopped macadamia nuts and serve with Citrus Mustard Vinaigrette (recipe follows).

Citrus Mustard Vinaigrette

½ cup canola oil
2 tablespoons fresh lemon juice
1 tablespoon fresh orange juice
2 teaspoons mustard (vinegar-free such
  as Coleman's®)

1 tablespoon barley malt syrup
¼ teaspon red pepper flakes (optional)
½ teaspoon sea salt

• Place all ingredients in a sealed container and shake vigorously to blend. Refrigerate if not using the day it is made.

This is called "Mystical" Minestrone because kids may choose the combination of vegetables and beans and pasta they'd like to have from the list below - so it changes each time it's made.

Mystical Minestrone

Serves 8-10

2 tablespoons EV olive oil
I cup diced onions
¼ teaspoon red pepper flakes (optional)
3 Italian all-natural chicken or turkey sausages, sliced (optional)
4 cloves garlic, minced
8 cups low-sodium chicken broth (vegetable broth if vegetarian minestrone)
I cup water
Veggie choices (see below)
Bean choices (see below)

½ cup chopped fresh basil
¼ cup chopped fresh, flat-leafed parsley
I teaspoon Herbes de Provence
I bay leaf
2 teaspoons sea salt
½ teaspoon freshly ground black pepper
I (28-ounce) can diced tomatoes and their juices
Pasta choices (see below)
Chopped fresh basil for topping

Veggie Choices: celery, carrots, green cabbage, kale, spinach, zucchini, red or green bell pepper, peas, green beans, asparagus (Total cups of chopped vegetables to be used - 4 cups)

Cooked Bean "Legume" Choices: edamame, kidney, garbanzo (chick peas), black, (Total cups of cooked beans to be used - 1¾ cups)

Pasta choices (Multigrain, Low Glycemic or Gluten-Free): spaghetti (broken into pieces), elbows, fiori, farfalle, orzo, ditalini (Total cups of dry pasta to be used - ⅔ cups)

- In a large stock pot, sauté onions, crushed red pepper flakes, and sausage slices in EV olive oil for 10 minutes, stirring occasionally with wooden spoon. Add the garlic and sauté for another 2 minutes. Add the broth and water; stir. Add the assorted vegetables, beans, and the herbs and spices. Bring to a boil, reduce heat and simmer for 15 minutes. Add the diced tomatoes and simmer for 10 minutes.

- In a separate pot, cook the pasta according to package directions (al dente), drain and place pasta in serving bowls. Ladle minestrone over pasta and serve topped with chopped fresh basil.

Here's another recipe suggestion from Kyle Picard. Anti- inflammatory avocados provide healthy fat. Creamy and smooth, this treat is packed with Vitamins B, E and K.

Extraordinary Mousse

Serves 3

2 ripe avocados
¼ cup unsweetened cocoa powder
⅛ teaspoon Ceylon cinnamon (optional)
¼ cup coconut nectar
2 teaspoons pure vanilla extract

- Place all ingredients in a food processor and mix until creamy and smooth. Serve immediately or spread into ice trays with Popsicle sticks and freeze for a frozen treat.

Authentic pizza, yeast-free, dairy-free and delicious! Note - this pizza cooks well on the "convection bake" setting if your oven has one and should always be cooked on a hot pizza stone.

Stone Pizza

Serves 4

½ batch Flying Saucer Bread dough (page 32)

EV olive oil

I package shredded vegetable mozzarella cheese

I½ cups Quick & Tasty Tomato Sauce (page 38)

I-2 fresh, fully-cooked, all-natural chicken sausage, sliced (such as spinach/garlic variety) or ⅓ pound of ground grass-fed bison

Roasted red and yellow bell pepper slices

Assorted olives, sliced

2 tablespoons chopped fresh (or ½ teaspoon dried) basil

½ teaspoon sea salt

Sprinkle of garlic powder

- Place large pizza stone in oven and preheat oven to 450°F for at least 25 minutes prior to cooking pizza. The stone must be very hot in order to properly cook this flatbread.

- Make ½ batch of Flying Saucer bread; knead dough for 5 minutes on well- floured surface (you will have to flour it often while kneading). Roll out to 12- inch diameter and let it sit on well-floured surface until oven is completely preheated. Remove hot stone from oven and transfer pizza shell to stone. Drizzle pizza dough with EV olive oil. Place pizza shell and stone back in oven and bake for 4 minutes. If large bubbles occur while it is baking, poke them down with the end of a wooden spoon. (Be careful – protect your eyes when you open the oven door!)

- Remove pizza stone with partially baked pizza from oven. Working quickly, top pizza shell with tomato sauce, cheese, chicken sausage slices or ground bison, peppers and olives. Sprinkle with seasonings. Place stone and pizza back in oven; bake an additional 10-12 minutes or until cheese is bubbly and slightly browned in places.

This is a great use for leftover sweet potatoes, and as always, if you have the Irish Soda Bread, Super Spelt Sandwich Bread, or Billowy Biscuits already made and frozen in sections in your freezer, you can just thaw as needed to make breadcrumbs.

Aloha Chicken Fingers with Sweet & Spicy Dipping Sauce

Serves 4

1½ cups Irish Soda Bread dried breadcrumbs (page 35) or other yeast-free dried breadcrumbs

½ cup flaxseed meal or amaranth flour

¼ cup sweet potato puree

¼ cup unsweetened applesauce or ¼ cup coconut nectar

1 tablespoon liquid aminos seasoning

1 large egg white, lightly beaten

¼ cup plus 2 tablespoons shredded unsweetened coconut

1 pound boneless, skinless chicken breast, rinsed, dried and cut into 'fingers'

Sea salt and freshly ground black pepper

- Preheat oven to 400°F. In a bowl, mix the breadcrumbs with the flour. Set aside. In a second shallow bowl, combine the sweet potato puree, applesauce or coconut nectar, liquid aminos seasoning, egg white, and coconut with a fork; set next to breadcrumbs mixture.

- Sprinkle both sides of the chicken with sea salt and black pepper. Dip the chicken into the sweet potato mixture and roll in the breadcrumb/flour mixture until completely coated.

- Place on parchment-lined baking sheet and bake in preheated oven for 15-18 minutes or until coating is nicely browned, turning once after 7 minutes. Serve with Sweet & Spicy Dipping Sauce.

Sweet & Spicy Dipping Sauce

2 tablespoons liquid aminos seasoning

1 tablespoon fresh lime juice

2 tablespoons coconut nectar

1 tablespoon mustard (vinegar-free such as Coleman's®)

- Combine ingredients in a small bowl and whisk until smooth.

Beets Me Salad

Serves 4

2 medium-sized beets, roasted, peeled and sliced
2 medium-sized red and/or yellow tomatoes, sliced
2 green onions, chopped
1 tablespoon chopped fresh mint
¼ cup EV olive oil
2 tablespoons lemon juice
1 teaspoon coarse sea salt

- Preheat oven to 400°F. To roast beets, scrub them with skins on and place them on aluminum foil. Drizzle with 1 teaspoon EV olive oil. Pocket the foil around beets, leaving top just slightly open; place on baking pan and bake until tender (about 1 hour). Remove beets from oven and wrap them tightly in their foil packets and chill for 30-45 minutes. Remove from refrigerator and peel by squeezing beets between your fingers – peeling should roll right off. Slice beets and set aside.

- On a round platter, arrange tomato and beet slices alternately. Top with chopped green onions and mint. Drizzle with olive oil and lemon juice and sprinkle with coarse sea salt.

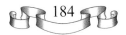

4th of July Fruit & Berry Salad

Serves 6

½ cup cold water

¼ cup coconut crystals or
   coconut nectar

2 tablespoons fresh lime juice

1 teaspoon finely chopped
   fresh mint

¼ teaspoon fennel or anise seeds

Pinch of sea salt

1 cup sliced fresh strawberries

1 cup cubed watermelon

1 cup sliced black or red seedless
   grapes

1 cup sliced nectarine

1 cup blackberries

1 cup blueberries

- In a small saucepan, bring the water, coconut crystals or nectar, lime juice, mint, and fennel or anise seeds to a boil for 2 minutes. Remove from heat and add the sea salt. Cover and cool the syrup completely.

- Rinse berries, drain and pat dry. Place the fruit and berries in a medium bowl and add the cooled syrup, coating thoroughly. Cover and chill for 1 hour, stirring occasionally. Stir and drain slightly just before serving.

Lemony Chicken Bites

Serves 6

3 boneless, skinless chicken breasts, cubed (1-inch)

⅓ cup fresh lemon juice

2 tablespoons liquid aminos seasoning

2 tablespoons mustard (vinegar-free such as Coleman's®)

1 teaspoon EV olive oil

2 tablespoons coconut nectar

2 cloves garlic, minced

2 tablespoons finely chopped shallot

2 tablespoons fresh (or 2 teaspoons dried) flat-leafed parsley

- Place all ingredients in a non-reactive bowl and marinate for 2 hours. Preheat oven to 400°F. Place marinated chicken on baking sheet lined with parchment paper. Bake for 4 minutes, brush chicken with marinade and bake another 4 minutes. Turn chicken and continue cooking for another 3 minutes. Try this with Spicy Rice Pilaf (page 142).

Kids will have a great time assembling these wraps!

Rainbow Wraps

Makes as many as you'd like!

Flying Saucer Bread (page 32) or other yeast-free flatbread or pita bread

Purple cabbage, finely shredded
Red and yellow bell peppers, very thinly sliced
Radish, very thinly sliced
Cucumber, very thinly sliced
Carrots, shredded
Green onions, finely chopped
Broccoli, finely chopped
Very fresh Microgreen sprouts (cilantro, arugula, or beet)
Terrific Tomato Dressing (page 201), or Tofu Cream Cheese Spread (page 43)

To Assemble Wrap

- Place the vegetables on the flatbread in the order of the rainbow spectrum (red, orange, yellow, green, indigo, violet). Drizzle with choice of dressings listed above.

- Roll up the rainbow wraps and cut in half to serve. If serving as appetizer, cut each wrap into 6 pieces.

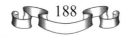

Christopher Bartorelli's mom, Marianne, sent us this recipe and by removing the corn and replacing it with avocados, it becomes totally safe for the kids and still so delicious! Antioxidants such as lycopene and beta-carotene are better absorbed with the healthy monounsaturated fat avocados have in abundance. Avocados are a good source of fiber, potassium, and Vitamins C, K, folate, and B6. Half an avocado has 160 calories, 15 grams of heart-healthy unsaturated fat, and only 2 grams of saturated fat. This alkaline vegetable is powerfully good for you.

Summer Side Salad

Serves 4

2 avocados, scooped from shell and diced
1 (15-ounce) can black beans, rinsed and drained
2 jalapeno peppers, seeded and finely chopped (optional)
1 pint cherry tomatoes (halved)
½ cup chopped red onion
2 teaspoons cumin
⅓ cup chopped fresh cilantro
1 teaspoon EV olive oil
Juice of 2 limes
Sea salt and freshly ground black pepper to taste

• Combine all ingredients in bowl and toss lightly. Serve immediately.

Tuna & 3-Bean Salad

Serves 2-4

3/4 pound fresh green and yellow wax beans, trimmed and cut into 1-inch pieces

2 tablespoons fresh lemon juice

1/2 teaspoon sea salt

1/8 teaspoon freshly ground black pepper

2 tablespoons EV olive oil

1 (15.5-ounce) can chick peas (garbanzo beans), rinsed and drained

1/2 small red or green onion, thinly sliced

1 (5-ounce) can solid white tuna packed in water, drained and broken into pieces

1/4 cup thinly sliced red bell or banana pepper

- Steam green beans until tender and still bright green (approximately 5 minutes). Drain, rinse under cold water to stop cooking; pat dry.

- In a large bowl, whisk together lemon juice, sea salt and black pepper. Add the remaining ingredients including the green and yellow wax beans. Fold gently to combine. Serve at room temperature or slightly chilled.

Amaranth is an excellent source of lysine, an important highly soluble amino acid (protein).

Harvest Moon Muffins

Makes 12 medium-sized muffins

½ cup white spelt flour

1 cup whole wheat flour

½ cup wheat semolina

2 tablespoons amaranth seeds

1½ teaspoons baking powder (cornstarch-free)

½ teaspoon baking soda

¼ teaspoon sea salt

2 teaspoons ground Ceylon cinnamon

½ teaspoon ground nutmeg

1 cup coconut crystals

1 cup canned or freshly cooked pumpkin

4 egg whites

½ cup canola oil

¼ cup soy milk

¼ cup unsweetened applesauce

½ cup raw pumpkin seeds

- Preheat oven to 400°F. Combine dry ingredients in a medium bowl. In a separate larger mixing bowl, blend pumpkin, egg whites, oil, soy milk and applesauce with a fork or spoon just until combined. Stir in flour mixture with a spoon, just until blended. Stir in pumpkin seeds. Spoon mixture evenly into 12 sections of medium-sized muffin tin lined with paper baking cups or greased with EV coconut oil. Pour water in the other 3 sections (halfway).

- Bake for 20 minutes or until a wooden toothpick or cake tester comes out clean. Cool in pan on wire rack for 5-10 minutes. Remove from pan and place directly on wire rack to cool.

Seasonal Goodies Fall

Allow 3 hours prep time (very simple!) prior to cooking this recipe. Serve this tasty vegetable medley as a side with brown rice, or with your favorite multigrain, low glycemic or gluten-free pasta or spoon it over the top of a baked potato.

Radical Ratatouille

Serves 4-6

2 medium globe eggplants cut into 1-inch dice

Sea salt

3 medium ripe tomatoes (not Romas), cored peeled (see below) and cut into 2-inch cubes

2 medium zucchini, seeded and cut into 1-inch dice

¼ cup EV olive oil

1 large onion, roughly diced

1 medium green or red bell pepper, cut into 1-inch dice

2 medium cloves garlic, minced

2 tablespoons chopped fresh (or 2 teaspoons dried), flat-leafed parsley

2 tablespoons chopped fresh (or 2 teaspoons dried) basil

1 tablespoon minced fresh (or 1 teaspoon dried) thyme

1 bay leaf

½ teaspoon freshly ground black pepper

- Place the diced eggplant into a large colander and sprinkle with 2 teaspoons sea salt. Toss to evenly distribute salt. Set over a bowl and let stand for 2 hours, stirring occasionally to help release water from eggplant. Rinse eggplant well with cold water and drain. Set eggplant on triple thickness of paper towels and with more paper towels, press down on eggplant firmly to soak up excess moisture. Set aside.

- To peel tomatoes, place cored tomatoes in a saucepan of boiling water three at a time. Boil tomatoes until the skin splits and begins to curl around core; about 20 seconds. Remove tomatoes with slotted spoon and place in a bowl of ice water to stop cooking process. The skin will easily peel away. Cut into 2-inch pieces and set aside.

- Preheat oven to 500°F. In a large bowl, toss the eggplant and zucchini with 2 tablespoons olive oil. Divide mixture onto two parchment or foil-lined baking pan and season with 1 teaspoon sea salt. Place baking sheets in oven and roast for 30-40 minutes, stirring every 10 minutes, until vegetables are well browned and very tender. Remove from oven and set aside.

- Meanwhile, place a Dutch oven or other heavy-bottomed pot on the stovetop; add 2 tablespoons olive oil over medium heat. Add the diced onions and green or red bell peppers; reduce heat to medium low and cook, stirring often, for 15 minutes. Add the garlic, herbs, black pepper and tomato pieces and cook for another 5 minutes.

- Add the eggplant and zucchini mixture to the Dutch oven; fold gently to coat, cook for 15 minutes. Serve warm.

For a change of pace, replace the chicken in this recipe with ground, grass- fed bison.

Shepherd's Pie

Serves 4-6

Prepare Tasty Mashed Taters recipe (page 200). Set aside.

Gravy

2 tablespoons ghee

3 tablespoons white spelt flour

1¼ cups low-sodium chicken broth

¼ teaspoon dried thyme

¼ teaspoon dried sage

¼ teaspoon granulated garlic

¼ teaspoon dried (ground) rosemary

¼ teaspoon red pepper flakes (optional)

¼ teaspoon sea salt

⅛ teaspoon freshly ground black pepper

• Place the ghee in a saucepan and heat until melted, add the flour and stir. Cook for 3 minutes, stirring occasionally. Add the remaining gravy ingredients; whisk and cook for 10 minutes on medium low, stirring often. Set aside.

To Prepare Chicken & Vegetables

2 cups peas, chopped green beans or carrots (or combination)

Sea salt and freshly ground black pepper

EV olive oil

I medium onion, diced

½ red bell pepper, diced

2 cooked chicken breasts, cubed, or I pound browned ground chicken or turkey

• Steam the peas, chopped green beans and/or carrots until just fork tender. Drain and set aside. Preheat a skillet on high and when it is quite hot, add 1 tablespoon EV olive oil. Add the diced onion and red bell pepper and stir fry for 3 minutes, turning often. Transfer the onions and pepper to a bowl and add the cubed or ground chicken; toss. Now you are ready to assemble the Shepherd's Pie.

To Assemble Pie

• Preheat oven to 400°F. Grease a casserole or pie dish with olive oil. Mix the gravy with the chicken mixture. Spread this mixture into the bottom of the casserole dish. Place the peas, green beans and/ or carrots on top of the meat mixture. Spread the mashed potatoes on top, bringing the potatoes all the way to the edge of the pan to seal the juices. Place the casserole dish on a baking sheet to catch any drippings, and bake for 30 minutes or just until potatoes begin to brown. Serve immediately.

The glycemic index in mashed potatoes is medium to high, but during and after chemotherapy, this soft, comforting vegetable may sometimes be the only food your child will eat. Keeping the skins on will help to retain 75% of the nutrients and fiber, thereby reducing the GI. (Turmeric's anti-inflammatory properties help to ease nausea.)

Tasty Mashed Taters

Serves 4-6

6 medium red potatoes, unpeeled, quartered

¼ cup roughly chopped yellow onion

⅓ cup each diced green, red and yellow bell peppers

½ cup rice or soy milk

¼ cup low-sodium chicken broth

3 tablespoons ghee

½ teaspoon sea salt

½ teaspoon ground turmeric

½ teaspoon freshly ground black pepper

Chopped fresh flat-leafed parsley for topping

- Fill bottom half of steamer pan with water. Place potatoes in top half of covered steamer pan with the chopped onion and peppers. Bring to a boil; reduce heat and steam on medium high until potatoes are soft when pierced with a fork (30 minutes), checking to be sure water does not boil away during steaming process. Drain and transfer steamed vegetables to a bowl. Mash and set aside, covered.

- Place rice or soy milk, chicken broth and ghee into a small saucepan and heat until ghee is mostly melted and mixture is warm, add salt, turmeric and black pepper; stir. Add this mixture to mashed potatoes a little at a time to desired consistency. Using an electric mixer beat the potatoes until light and fluffy. Serve sprinkled with chopped fresh parsley.

This is a great dish for using up that leftover Thanksgiving turkey.

Tom Turkey Wrap with Terrific Tomato Dressing

Serves 4

1 large head Romaine lettuce, chopped

8 radishes, sliced

1 cucumber, sliced

½ cup shredded carrots

½ small red onion, thinly sliced

2 cups chopped or shredded cooked turkey

- Place all ingredients equally into 4 large yeast-free flat-breads such as Flying Saucer Bread (page 32). Drizzle with Terrific Tomato Dressing and serve.

Terrific Tomato Dressing

2 fresh Roma tomatoes

2 tablespoons EV olive oil

½ teaspoon sea salt

¼ teaspoon freshly ground black pepper

1 small garlic clove, minced

2 tablespoons fresh, flat-leafed parsley, chopped

- Quarter the tomatoes and place all ingredients in a food processor and pulse until smooth. Refrigerate until ready to use.

Angels' Answers

In the life of most kids with cancer, deaths of beloved friends who also had cancer are experienced. This doesn't always mean that they are gone forever and lost as friends. Many of my friends have become Angels. Although I miss them greatly, I still believe that they are in my life, just in a different way.

Many of the friends that I lost were very passionate about food and cooking, as am I. Without the help from the spirit world, this cookbook would never have come together. I especially believe that my friend Kyle is responsible for finding the special people who are helping me with this cookbook. But the other Angel Knights are helping in their own ways. I am honored to share their stories and some of their favorite recipes with you. They will always remain alive in our hearts and memories.

- Lexie

Richard William Hoffman

(Sir Ricky the Relentless)
December 9, 1997 ~ November 6, 2009

Sir Ricky the Relentless, Knight of Reflection, was all about reflecting love. He adored going on adventures around Magical Moon Farm looking for treasures with his fellow knights. When it came time for Ricky to choose a knight's mission, it was no wonder that his included an adventure! Ricky wanted to build a path made of heart-shaped rocks that would lead to Hope Castle at the Magical Moon Farm. People from everywhere searched for heart-shaped rocks to help Ricky build his Path of Hope. Because Ricky loved M&M® cookies, Magical Moon Foundation has declared December 9th our official M&M® Cookie Day.

Ricky Hoffman enjoyed sharing M&M® Cookies with everyone he loved. It's now a tradition at Magical Moon Farm to honor Ricky by continuing to share M&M® Cookies on very special occasions only!

Ricky's M&M® Cookies

Makes 24-36 Cookies

⅔ cup ghee, softened
¼ cup canola oil
1½ cups coconut crystals
2 teaspoons pure vanilla extract
4 egg whites
1¼ cups white spelt flour

1 cup whole wheat flour
1⅛ teaspoons baking soda
1 teaspoon sea salt
1½ cups plain M&M®s (preferably dark chocolate)

- In a large mixing bowl, cream the ghee, canola oil and coconut crystals with an electric mixer until creamy. Add vanilla extract, followed by the egg whites. Beat for 1 minute. In a separate bowl, combine the flour, baking soda and salt. Add to the wet mixture and beat until well combined. Do not add the M&M®'s at this time. Chill cookie batter for at least 1 hour.

- Preheat oven to 375°F. Form balls with a small ice cream scoop or a tablespoon and arrange well apart on an ungreased baking sheet. Bake in oven for 9 minutes. Remove from oven and quickly add M&M®s (7 per cookie – but one cookie with 10 M&M®s in honor of Ricky!) by just slightly pressing them into the cookie. Bake for another 3-5 minutes. Remove from oven and let cool for 5 minutes before transferring to a wire rack to cool.

Joshua Andrew Gehman

February 20, 2001 ~ January 11, 2011

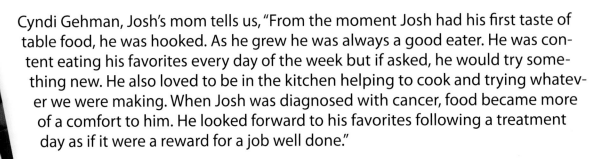

Cyndi Gehman, Josh's mom tells us, "From the moment Josh had his first taste of table food, he was hooked. As he grew he was always a good eater. He was content eating his favorites every day of the week but if asked, he would try something new. He also loved to be in the kitchen helping to cook and trying whatever we were making. When Josh was diagnosed with cancer, food became more of a comfort to him. He looked forward to his favorites following a treatment day as if it were a reward for a job well done."

We've dedicated our 'Veggie Macaroni & Cheese' recipe (below) to Josh because it is a classic comfort food with a brand new twist.

The vegetables and macadamia nuts are the "cheese" in this very tasty dish.

Veggie Macaroni & Cheese

Serves 4

1 cup multigrain, low glycemic or gluten-free elbow macaroni pasta

2-3 slices of Irish Soda Bread (page 35) or other yeast-free bread, torn into large pieces

4 tablespoons ghee (divided)

2 tablespoons chopped shallots

1 cup peeled & chopped potatoes

½ cup chopped carrots

⅓ cup chopped onions

1 cup water

¼ cup chopped raw macadamia nuts

1 teaspoon sea salt

¼ teaspoon minced garlic

¼ teaspoon mustard (vinegar-free such as Coleman's®)

1 tablespoon fresh lemon juice

¼ teaspoon freshly ground black pepper

¼ teaspoon paprika

Veggie Macaroni & Cheese, continued

- Cook 1 cup elbow macaroni according to package directions. Rinse, drain and set aside.

- In a food processor, make breadcrumbs by pulsing the bread and only 2 tablespoons of the ghee to a medium-fine texture. Set aside.

- Preheat oven to 350°F. In a saucepan, add shallots, potatoes, carrots, onions, and water, and bring to a boil. Cover pan and simmer 15 minutes, or until vegetables are soft.

- In a blender, process the nuts, sea salt, garlic, remaining 2 tablespoons ghee, mustard, lemon juice, black pepper, and paprika. Add softened vegetables and cooking water to the blender and process until perfectly smooth to make the cheese sauce.

- In a large bowl, toss the cooked pasta and blended cheese sauce until the pasta is completely coated. Spread mixture into a casserole dish and sprinkle with prepared breadcrumbs. Bake for 30 minutes or until the cheese sauce is bubbling and the breadcrumbs are golden brown. Serve immediately.

Devon Marie Lam

January 24, 2003 ~ December 5, 2008

Angela Lam, Devon's mom, tells us, "Devon not only loved sampling different kinds of cuisines but she also enjoyed food shopping and preparing food with her Mommy. Her favorite dish to help prepare was whole grain pancakes and she of course consumed as many as she could with a grin from ear to ear. She also looked forward to going out to eat. Her "go to" dish was pasta with chicken and broccoli in garlic-infused olive oil. Devon was happiest when she was sitting around a table surrounded by those she loved and great food!"

Here's a pancake recipe in honor of one of Devon's favorites.

Power Pancakes with
Bionic Blueberry Syrup

Serves 4

1 cup whole spelt flour
1 cup oat flour
2 tablespoons baking powder
  (cornstarch-free)
1 teaspoon sea salt
¼ cup coconut crystals

1 teaspoon pure vanilla extract
4 egg whites
1½ cups rice or soy milk
⅓ cup canola oil
2 tablespoons ghee, melted

Bionic Blueberry Syrup (page 30) or coconut nectar for drizzling

- Sift flours with baking powder and salt into a mixing bowl. Add remaining ingredients and beat by hand until just mixed. Drop by ice cream scoop onto hot, canola-oil greased cast iron griddle. Cook until underside is golden brown and bubbles appear over surface. Turn and cook until underside is golden brown. Top with ghee or natural buttery substitute and drizzle with Bionic Blueberry Syrup or coconut nectar.

Kasey Ryan Radford

January 1, 1998 ~ February 4, 2009

Amy Radford, Kasey's mom says, "Our Kasey loved to help others wherever and whenever possible. Cooking was definitely one of his favorite passions, especially if he was preparing something for someone else. He had his own set of cookbooks, small appliances and an apron to boot. Kasey lived to serve and whenever friends or family would visit, he would offer up a hot grilled cheese sandwich or a fresh cup of cocoa. Our Kasey aimed to please. He was such a treasure and his helping hand is missed each day in our kitchen!"

Here is the Moon Spoon Team's version of Kasey's Grilled Cheese Sandwiches.

Kasey's Grilled Cheese Sandwich

Makes 2 Sandwiches

Softened ghee

4 slices Super Spelt Sandwich Bread (page 42) or other yeast-free bread

4 slices vegetable Swiss cheese

Handful shredded vegetable mozzarella cheese

Sliced tomato (optional)

Sliced red onion (optional)

Mustard (vinegar-free such as Coleman's®), (optional)

- Spread softened ghee on outside of each of the four slices of bread. Assemble sandwiches (2 slices of Swiss cheese and ½ cup shredded mozzarella cheese on each sandwich along with tomato, onion and mustard if preferred) and place on heated skillet and cook slowly on both sides until cheese is softened and bread is nicely toasted.

John Matthew Shapiro

January 23, 2005 ~August 5, 2011

His Mom, Nancy, tell us, "Food, friends, and fun… for John Shapiro, these three things naturally went together. Nothing made him happier than sharing a tasty treat with friends. In fact, John used food to make new friends. At camp he would man the reception desk and always had something to share with the other kids. John would delight in their smiles when they took one of his snacks. At home, no one liked a party more than John. He always had a job in mind; filling your glass with ice, serving hors d'oeuvres, or helping plan the meal. John understood how food is interwoven with life and that sharing a meal with family and friends makes any occasion better. John loved food! Thank goodness John's illness did not take away his love of food. He was all about the food all the time!"

Here's a tasty snack we've dedicated to John because he especially loved snacks.

Sassy Salsa with Toasted Triangles

Serves 4

3 ripe tomatoes, chopped, seeds removed, drained

2 Jalapeño peppers, finely chopped

1 small red onion or 4 green onions, finely chopped

2 tablespoons fresh cilantro, finely chopped

Juice and zest of one lime

1 small clove garlic, minced

½ teaspoon cumin

Sea salt and freshly ground black pepper to taste

- Mix all salsa ingredients and set aside.

Flatbread triangles

Chili powder

Cumin

Sea Salt

EV Olive oil

- Preheat oven to 350°F. Cut Flying Saucer Bread (plain or Southwestern version), (page 32) or other yeast- free flatbread into triangles and if they are not already seasoned, sprinkle with chili powder, cumin, sea salt & EV olive oil. Place on parchment or foil-lined baking pan and bake for 10-15 minutes or until very crispy. Scoop the salsa with the baked flatbread triangles.

Bridget Eileen Sweeney

August 17, 1998 ~ January 14, 2010

Bridget was not a knight of the Magical Moon, but she did have a mission and that was to bring joy to her family and friends through her love of cooking. Bridget's mom, Cheryl, tells us, "Bridget loved to bake from the moment she was able to stand on a chair and reach the kitchen counter. As a toddler she would beg to bake cookies or brownies so she could crack the eggs and stir. By the time she was six she refused to use a packaged mix – too simple and boring! When she was in treatment and not feeling well, the lure of baking was one of the few things that could move her off the couch and put a smile on her face. Her chocolate chip cookies were her specialty, and always disappeared quickly at bake sales. She collected her own special pans, scoops, baking mats and jars of colored sprinkles. Her motto was "a dessert could never have enough sprinkles of chocolate". She would make molded chocolates to decorate her special chocolate torte. Despite our best efforts to get her to gain some weight, she never really ate her creations. It was all the job of creating and the pleasure of sharing that made her happy. Chocolate chip cookies for her classmates, Boston cream cupcakes for her uncle, bread pudding for her brother… she made them all with love."

In honor of Bridget, here's one of her favorite recipes, re-touched.

Bridget's Chocolate Chip Cookies

Makes 2 dozen cookies

1 cup coconut crystals

⅔ cup ghee, softened

2 teaspoons pure vanilla extract

4 egg whites

1 tablespoon soy or rice milk

1 cup white spelt flour

1 cup whole wheat flour

¾ teaspoon baking soda

1 teaspoon sea salt

2 cups bittersweet chocolate chips

- Preheat oven to 350°F. In a large mixing bowl using an electric mixer, combine coconut crystals and ghee until well combined. Add the vanilla extract, egg whites and soy or rice milk. Mix well. In a separate bowl, combine the flours, baking soda and sea salt. With mixer on low or by hand, add dry ingredients to the wet mixture and beat for 1 minute, scraping sides of bowl occasionally. Fold in the chocolate chips and using a medium ice cream scoop or heaping tablespoon, drop onto parchment-lined baking sheet. Bake for 15 minute. Remove from baking sheet and transfer to wire rack to cool.

Desserts

Desserts are special, rare treats. Always be sure to check with your nutritionist and health care provider to be sure it is okay to satisfy your sweet tooth.

Beach Day Cookies

Makes 16-20 Cookies

¼ cup ghee, softened

¼ cup EV coconut oil

1 cup soy nut butter

1 cup coconut crystals

¼ cup unsweetened applesauce

2 egg whites

1 teaspoon pure vanilla extract

1¼ cups white spelt flour

¾ cup whole wheat flour

½ teaspoon baking soda

¼ teaspoon sea salt

- In a mixing bowl, using an electric mixer, blend ghee, EV coconut oil, soy nut butter, coconut crystals, applesauce, egg whites and vanilla extract for 1 minute, scraping sides of bowl occasionally. Combine dry ingredients in a separate bowl. With mixer on low, combine the dry ingredients with the ghee mixture and mix for just 30 seconds, scraping sides of bowl occasionally. Cover batter with plastic wrap and chill for 1 hour.

- Preheat oven to 375°F. Form dough into 1-inch balls and place 2 inches apart on ungreased or parchment-lined baking sheet. Flatten slightly with floured fork (crisscross pattern). Bake for 12-14 minutes. (For crispier cookies, bake for 16 minutes.) Remove from oven and transfer to wire rack to cool.

Zucchini, summer squash or pumpkin may be used in this recipe. If using fresh instead of canned squash or pumpkin, peel and steam until tender, drain well and mash (do this before measuring the 2 cups needed because it shrinks down considerably, so start with at least 4 cups fresh, raw squash or pumpkin).

Chocolate Pumpkin Cupcakes

Makes 20 medium or 10 large cupcakes

¼ cup ghee, softened
¾ cup canola oil
1⅔ cups coconut crystals
4 egg whites
1 teaspoon pure vanilla extract
½ cup rice or soy milk with 2 teaspoons
  lemon juice
1½ cups whole wheat pastry flour

1 cup white spelt flour
½ teaspoon sea salt
¼ cup cocoa (sifted)
1 teaspoon Ceylon cinnamon
2 cups fresh or canned cooked pumpkin,
  zucchini or summer squash
½ cup bittersweet chocolate chips
½ cup raw, unsalted pumpkin seeds

- Preheat oven to 325°F. In a large mixing bowl using electric mixer, combine the ghee, canola oil and coconut crystals on medium speed for 1 minute. Add the egg whites and vanilla extract and beat for 1 minute. Combine the dry ingredients in a separate bowl. With mixer on low, add dry ingredients to oil mixture alternately with the rice or soy milk (and lemon) and mix for 30 seconds, scraping sides of bowl occasionally. Add the squash or pumpkin and beat on medium speed for 1 more minute.

- Line cupcake tins with paper baking cups. Fill to three quarters full with batter. Top with chocolate chips and pumpkin seeds and bake for approximately 22-25 minutes or until toothpick inserted in center of cupcake comes out clean.

Desserts

Half Moon Macadamia Nut Cookies

Makes 10-12 cookies

½ cup fresh raw macadamia nuts, toasted and finely ground
½ cup ghee, softened
⅓ cup coconut crystals
2 egg whites
¼ teaspoon coarse sea salt
1 tablespoon finely grated lemon zest
½ teaspoon lemon juice
½ cup white spelt flour
½ cup whole wheat flour
¼ teaspoon baking soda
1 cup bittersweet chocolate chips

- Preheat oven to 350°F. Place macadamia nuts on a parchment or foil-lined baking pan and bake for 6 minutes. Remove nuts from oven, cool and grind in food processor; set aside. Do not turn off oven.

- In a large bowl using an electric mixer, beat ghee and coconut crystals on medium high for 2 minutes until light and fluffy. Add egg whites and sea salt; beat until combined. Add lemon zest and lemon juice and stir. Fold in the cooled macadamia nuts. In a separate bowl, combine the flours, baking soda and sea salt. With mixer on low, combine the flour mixture with the ghee mixture for 30 seconds, occasionally scraping sides of bowl. Form dough into a 4½-inch long log, wrap in plastic wrap and freeze for 30 minutes. Cut into ¼-inch slices, transfer slices to two parchment-lined baking sheets. Bake until edges are golden, 12-14 minutes, rotating sheets halfway through. Let cookies cool completely on wire rack.

- Place water in bottom of a double boiler pan and place chocolate chips in top of double boiler. Bring water to a boil, reduce heat to medium; stir chocolate until melted and turn off heat. Dip half of each cookie into chocolate and place dipped cookies on parchment or wax paper-lined baking sheet and chill in refrigerator until set – about 30 minutes. Wrap cookies and keep them in a cool place.

Desserts

Say "pick-apart-a-pink-pomegranate" three times really fast!

Mighty Bites for Knights

Makes 24 Cookies

¼ cup plus 2 tablespoons ghee (softened)

½ cup canola oil

2 cups coconut crystals

4 egg whites

1 teaspoon pure vanilla extract

¾ cup unbleached, all-purpose flour

¾ cup whole wheat flour

1 teaspoon baking soda

1 teaspoon ground Ceylon cinnamon

½ teaspoon sea salt

3 cups rolled oats, old-fashioned, uncooked

2 tablespoons wheat germ

Fruit of 2 pomegranates

1 cup bittersweet chocolate chips

½ cup raw macadamia nuts, chopped

- Preheat oven to 375°F. In a large bowl using an electric mixer on medium speed, beat the ghee, canola oil and coconut crystals until well blended. Add the egg whites and vanilla extract and beat again for 1 minute. In a separate bowl, combine the flours, baking soda, Ceylon cinnamon, and sea salt; add dry ingredients to the ghee mixture and beat on low speed for 1 minute, scraping sides of bowl occasionally. Add the oats and wheat germ and stir. Fold in the pomegranate fruit, chocolate chips and macadamia nuts.

- Drop by ice cream scoop or large spoonfuls onto a baking sheet covered with parchment paper. Cook for 15 minutes or until golden brown but still soft. Cool on wire rack.

Champion No-Bake Cookies

Makes 12-16 cookies

1 cup plus 2 tablespoons coconut crystals
½ cup ghee
½ cup rice or soy milk
¼ cup cocoa, sifted

- Place all ingredients in a medium saucepan and bring to a full rolling boil. Once boiling, cook for exactly 3 minutes, stirring constantly. Remove from heat and add:

1 teaspoon pure vanilla extract
2 tablespoons soy nut butter
2½-3 cups rolled oats, old-fashioned, uncooked

- Drop by heaping tablespoonful onto parchment or foil-lined baking pan and chill.

Desserts

Don't forget to have the Gooey Orange Glaze all made by the time the cupcakes come out of the oven!

Orange Poppy Seed Cupcakes

Makes 20-22 medium cupcakes

Cupcakes

1¼ cups white spelt flour
1¼ cups oat flour
1 teaspoon baking powder
½ teaspoon baking soda
½ teaspoon sea salt
¼ cup ghee, softened
1½ cups coconut crystals

½ cup canola oil
4 egg whites
Zest of two oranges
½ cup fresh orange juice
2 tablespoons poppy seeds
½ cup soy or rice milk

- Preheat oven to 350°F. Line cupcake tins with paper baking cups. In a medium bowl, combine flours, baking powder, baking soda, and salt. In a large mixing bowl, cream ghee with coconut crystals until it looks like paste. Add the oil, egg whites, orange zest and juice, and poppy seeds. Blend well. With mixer on low speed, add the soy or rice milk alternately with the dry ingredients. Increase speed to medium and beat for just 30 seconds.

- Fill cupcake papers three quarters full. Bake for 20-22 minutes or until toothpick inserted in center comes out clean. While cupcakes are still hot, and before removing cupcakes from tin, poke seven holes in the top of each cupcake with a toothpick, and top each cupcake with 2 teaspoons Gooey Orange Glaze. Transfer cupcakes to wire rack to cool.

Gooey Orange Glaze

1 cup fresh orange juice
2 tablespoons orange zest
¾ cup coconut crystals

- Fifteen minutes before cupcakes have finished cooking, combine glaze ingredients in a small saucepan. Bring to a boil. Reduce heat and simmer 5 minutes. Remove from heat. Let cool another 10 minutes.

Desserts

Chia seeds are very high in Omega 3 fatty acids and they help to hydrate the body. Spelt flour contains very little gluten and will break down easily if over-handled. That's why low-speed electric or hand-mixing is always recommended when cooking with spelt.

Pumpkin Chocolate Chip Cookies

Makes 24 Cookies

1¼ cup canned pumpkin

1 cup coconut crystals

½ cup canola oil

2 egg whites

2 cups white spelt flour

2 teaspoons chia seeds

2 teaspoons baking powder (cornstarch-free)

2 teaspoons ground Ceylon cinnamon

½ teaspoon sea salt

1 teaspoon baking soda

2 teaspoons soy or rice milk

2 teaspoons pure vanilla extract

2 cups bittersweet chocolate chips

- Preheat oven to 350°F. In a mixing bowl using an electric mixer on medium speed, combine pumpkin, coconut crystals, canola oil and egg whites for 1 minute. In another bowl, combine flour, chia seeds, baking powder, Ceylon cinnamon, salt and baking soda. Add dry ingredients to wet ingredients along with soy or rice milk and vanilla extract. Mix on low speed for 30 seconds. Fold in chocolate chips.

- Drop by teaspoonfuls onto a baking sheet lined with parchment paper. Bake for 10-12 minutes. Remove cookies from pan and place on wire rack to cool.

Desserts

If you use spelt flour for this recipe, mix by hand or on low speed of electric mix to accommodate its low gluten content. Try this with blueberries too, using Bionic Blueberry Syrup (page 30).

Strawberry Moat Cake

Serves 9

Cake

2¼ cups white spelt flour

4 teaspoons baking powder
  (cornstarch-free)

1 teaspoon sea salt

1 cup plus 2 tablespoons soy or rice milk

2 teaspoons pure vanilla extract

6 large egg whites

⅔ cup ghee, softened

⅔ cup coconut crystals

- Preheat oven to 350°F. Grease bottom and sides of a square (9 x 9) cake pan with EV coconut oil. Combine flour, baking powder, and salt in bowl. In a separate bowl, whisk together soy or rice milk, vanilla extract, and egg whites for 2 minutes.

- With electric mixer on high speed, combine ghee and coconut crystals until smooth, about 3 minutes. Add flour mixture and milk mixture alternately in two batches while beating by hand for 1 minute or on low speed of electric mixture for 30 seconds, scraping sides of bowl occasionally. Pour batter into prepared pan and bake 30-35 minutes or until toothpick inserted in center comes out clean. Poke about 50 holes in top of cake, using wooden skewers (better than toothpicks because they're bigger around). Set aside.

Strawberry Topping

3 cups fresh or frozen strawberries, sliced

⅔ cup coconut nectar

1 teaspoon lemon juice

Pinch of sea salt

1 tablespoon kudzu root starch or
  arrowroot starch

2 tablespoons cold water

- In a small saucepan, combine strawberries, coconut nectar, lemon juice and sea salt. Place over medium heat. Mix starch with water. Add to strawberry mixture and bring to a boil. Reduce heat and simmer until thickened, stirring often.

- Remove from heat and pour hot, thickened Strawberry Topping over top of cake. Serve warm or cold.

Special Thanks

First and foremost, I want to thank my family. Your love makes me strong and you are my heroes. To my fellow Knights of the Magical Moon - including the angels - thank you for your friendship and your awesome support of my mission. And to their brave parents, I'm especially thankful to you for your enthusiasm for *Lexie's Gift*.

I'm so grateful to you, Dr. Mark Mincolla, for your expert advice and nutritional guidance and for teaching us that our immune system is an army of soldiers fighting to keep us healthy – and that eating right fuels its mission.

Sincere thanks to Wilma Goodhue and Friendship Home for letting us use your certified kitchen to conduct our first "cook-off" of some of the recipes – we had a blast! Thank you Lisa Segal and Segal Media Productions for filming and "You Tubing" our cooking event at Le Cordon Bleu Culinary Institute, and to Rafael Castaneda, Betsy Swan, Chef McCullough and the many wonderful student chefs who provided a happy cooking day to remember forever. Many thanks, LCB! We are also extremely grateful for our very talented book designer, Jean Cousins, www.jeancousins.com and for our caring and thorough recipe proofreaders, Sherri Nisbett, Suzanne Sirois and Clayton Manzo.

This cookbook could not have been done without the Moon Spoon Team: Georgia Manzo Joachim, Betty Greene, Alice Williams (my mom), and Donna Green, Founder and Executive Director of The Magical Moon Foundation – all of whom have been working with me on this cookbook since January of 2011. Betty brought organization, enthusiasm and great questions and answers to the table and helped test the recipes and offer needed advice when we were headed down the wrong path. Georgia helped with the writing of this cookbook, and transformed traditional recipes to make them safer for kids with cancer, with guidance provided by Dr. Mark Mincolla, and driven by her love for kids and for cooking. My mom provided unconditional support for my mission along with lots of hugs and laughs (walk away from the blender!) and wisdom beyond words. Her optimism lights the way for me. Donna guides me spiritually - just as she led the Moon Spoon Team - with quiet grace and the power of her love and belief in the knights who shine over this mission and inspire me to be the most I can be. If it were not for Donna and the Magical Moon

Foundation, this important and groundbreaking cookbook would not exist and be made available to the parents and kids for whom it was written.

And finally, I want to especially thank the New England Teamsters Joint Council 10 for providing the funding for the first edition of *Lexie's Gift*. Their support and generosity made my dream a reality!

I am forever grateful to all of you for your love and support and for believing in my mission to create a cookbook for kids with cancer.

– Lexie Williams

Lexie's Gift

A COOKBOOK FOR KIDS LIVING WITH CANCER

Afterword

Nutritional Needs after Cancer - Note to Parents

Your child's journey forward following cancer and treatment should be continued with your health care providers and nutritionist. Organic foods, high in well balanced essential fatty acids - Omega 3, Omega 6 and Omega 9 oils - such as are in avocados, olives, chia seeds, hemp seeds, fresh walnuts, almonds, extra virgin olive oil, cold water fish such as salmon, trout and tuna, soy nut butter, lean meats, legumes, fruits, vegetables, and liquid nutritional products and supplements are all beneficial.

Consider putting some fresh blueberries, chia seeds or hulled raw hemp seeds in your child's morning oatmeal, or provide a handful of seeds or macadamia nuts for a snack. Continue to serve the recipes in this cookbook, especially those with ingredients listed above. Spread some mashed avocado drizzled with fresh lime juice in a Southwest-seasoned chicken/vegetable taco (yeast- free) topped with vegetable pepper jack cheese, or just get creative with the healthy choices outlined in this cookbook and ask your child to choose and help prepare the recipes within.

Pack some vegetable cheeses and munch-able green vegetables like sugar snap peas and broccoli when you take your kids to their favorite restaurant so they can have it with an egg white omelet or with grilled chicken breast. Pack the Magical Moon Energy Bars for a quick and healthy snack in the car, or grab some soup out of the freezer, heat it and put it in your thermos for a healthy and wholesome lunch on the road along with a Billowy Biscuit. Ask your child for healthy snacks-on-the-go ideas!

And as you continue to help your child celebrate life, please also know that she or he is not alone, and that The Magical Moon Foundation, Nurturing and Empowering Children with Cancer, is just a click away – www.magicalmoon.org.

Sources

Alden, Lori. (n.d.) The Cook's Thesaurus. Starch Thickeners. Retrieved from URL: *http://www.foodsubs. com/ThickenStarch.html*

Alterman, Tabitha. (December 2011/January 2012 edition) How to Afford Better Food. *Mother Earth News Magazine, Ogden Publications, Topeka, KS: 37-42*

American Cancer Society. (Last Medical Review 09/22/2011, Last Revised, 09/22/2011) Fatigue. Retrieved from URL: *http://www.cancer.org/treatment/treatmentsandsideeffects/physicalsideeffects/fatigue/fatigueinpeoplewithcancer*

American Cancer Society. (Last Medical Review 01/17/2013, Last Revised 01/17/2013) Phytochemicals. Retrieved from URL: *http://www.cancer.org/Treatment/TreatmentsandSideEffects/ComplementaryandAlternativeMedicine/HerbsVitaminsandMinerals/Phytochemicals*

American Cancer Society. (Last Medical Review 01/17/2013, Last Revised 01/17/2013) What Children with Cancer Need: Nutrients. Retrieved from URL: *http://www.cancer.org/treatment/childrenandcancer/whenyourchildhascancer/nutritionforchildrenwithcancer/nutrition-for-children-with-cancerwhat-children-with-cancer-need*

Children's Brain Tumor Foundation., (2007). A Resource Guide for Parents of Children with Brain or Spinal Cord Tumors. *CBTF Publications, New York. 4th Edition*

Davis, Annette, CN. (2011) EIMC (Endobiogenic Integrative Medical Center). Cancer Dietary Guidelines. Retrieved from URL: *http://www.eimcenter.com/CancerDietaryGuidelines.pdf*

Sources

Diabetes Advocates. (2007) (Diabetes Wellness Clinic of America). Sugars and Substitutes with their Glycemic Index. Retrieved from URL: *http://www.diabetesadvocates.info/LearningCenter/Food%20 Nutrition%20Fatcs/AgaveNectar.html*

Eldridge, Lynne, M.D. (Updated February 15, 2013). What is Cancer Fatigue? Why Am I So Tired? Retrieved from URL: *http://www.lungcancer.about.com/od/livingwithlungcancer/a/cancerfatigue.htm.*

Hailey's Wish. (n.d.) What Are Mitochondria? Retrieved from: URL: *http://www.haileyswish.org/medical-info/#1*

Mincolla, Mark, Ph.D. (August 29, 2013) Fighting Cancer Naturally Retrieved from URL: *http://www.mark-mincolla.com/site/fighting-cancer-naturally/*

Nutrition Data.com. Self Nutrition Data, Know What You Eat. Nutrition Facts. Retrieved from URL: *http:// nutritiondata.self.com/*

Oz, Mehmet, M.D. (February 15, 2011) Dr. Oz's Prevention Power Pack. Retrieved from URL: *http://www. doctoroz.com/videos/prevention-power-pack?page=3*

Sisson, Mark. (October 20, 2011) Mark's Daily Apple, Primal Living in the Modern World. Mitochondria. Retrieved from URL: *http://www.marksdailyapple.com/managing-your-mitochondria-nutrients-and-supplements/#axzz2fRZhohq1*

Trum Hunter, Beatrice. (2006). A Whole Foods Primer, A Comprehensive, Instructive, and Enlightening Guide to the World of Whole Foods. *California, Basic Health Publications, Inc.: A Cornucopia of Vegetables, Beyond Nutrients: Phytochemicals 1:3-6.*

Recipe Index

Recipe Index

Recipe Index

Recipe Index

Recipe Index